The SYBEX Prompter™ Series

LOTUS 1-2-3® INSTANT REFERENCE

Release 2.2

Greg Harvey
and
Kay Yarborough Nelson

San Francisco • Paris • Düsseldorf • Soest

Acquisitions Editor: Dianne King
Series Editor: James A. Compton
Copy Editor: Michael L. Wolk
Technical Editor: Aziz Khatri
Word Processor: Chris Mockel
Series Book Designer: Ingrid Owen
Production Artist: Charlotte Carter
Screen Graphics: Delia Brown
Typesetter: Winnie Kelly
Proofreader: Ed Lin
Indexer: Paul Geisert
Cover Design: Thomas Ingalls + Associates

An earlier version of this book was published under the title *Lotus 1-2-3 Instant Reference* copyright 1988 SYBEX Inc.

Library of Congress Card Number: 89-63172
ISBN 0-89588-635-9
Manufactured in the United States of America
10 9 8 7 6 5

The SYBEX Prompter Series

We've designed the SYBEX Prompter Series to meet the evolving needs of software users, who want essential information presented in an accessible format. Our best authors have distilled their expertise into compact *Instant Reference* books you can use to look up the precise use of any command—its syntax, available options, and operation. More than just summaries, these books also provide realistic examples and insights into effective usage drawn from our authors' wealth of experience.

The SYBEX Prompter Series also includes these titles:

Lotus 1-2-3 Instant Reference
Greg Harvey and Kay Yarborough Nelson

WordPerfect Instant Reference
Greg Harvey and Kay Yarborough Nelson

WordPerfect 5 Instant Reference
Greg Harvey and Kay Yarborough Nelson

dBASE Instant Reference
Alan Simpson

dBASE IV User's Instant Reference
Alan Simpson

dBASE IV Programmer's Instant Reference
Alan Simpson

DOS Instant Reference
Greg Harvey and Kay Yarborough Nelson

HyperTalk Instant Reference
Greg Harvey

WordStar Instant Reference
David J. Clark

Ventura Instant Reference
Matthew Holtz

Hard Disk Instant Reference
Judd Robbins

Excel Instant Reference
William J. Orvis

AutoCAD Instant Reference
George Omura

Acknowledgments

Thanks are due to the following people: at SYBEX, Dr. R. S. Langer and Alan Oakes for furnishing the inspiration for this series over Dim Sum; Tanya Kucak, for her skillful copy edit of the original version of this book; Brian Atwood, for writing the additional material on Release 2.2; and, at Lotus Development Corporation, Alexandra Trevelyan and Susan Earabino for providing timely information and current software.

TABLE OF CONTENTS

Introduction

The idea behind this book is simple: When you are stymied by a function that does not work as you intended or a command that produces unpredicted results, or if you want a quick refresher about a certain procedure, you need a single source of information that can help you quickly solve the problem at hand so that you can get on with your work.

The *Lotus 1-2-3 Instant Reference* is intended to supply just that: to give you in as short a space as possible the essential information necessary to get the most from Lotus 1-2-3's numerous features—the basic commands as well as the built-in functions that you may not use on a daily basis. It covers both Release 2 and Release 2.2 of the program; commands found only in Release 2.2 of Lotus 1-2-3 are denoted by 2.2 in the entry heading.

If you find that your work takes you beyond the scope of the quick advice this book gives you, you may want to consider the *The Complete Lotus 1-2-3 Release 2.2 Handbook* by Greg Harvey (SYBEX, 1989); this reference book covers all aspects of Lotus 1-2-3 in detail.

How This Book Is Organized

This book is divided into two parts: Chapters 1–8 give you entries for each command available when you press the slash (/) key, and Chapters 9–17 give entries for each of the built-in @ functions found in the program.

The Lotus 1-2-3 command reference entries in the first part are presented in the same order as they are found when you access the menu system by pressing the slash key (/):

Worksheet Range Copy Move File Print Graph Data System Add-In Quit

Each command entry gives you the command name, a short description of what the command does, the key sequence used to access the command, and any command options and how to use them, followed by examples, special comments, and references to related commands, if applicable. All submenu options attached to any of the commands on the Main Menu are discussed in the general section on the command in question and are presented in the order in which they appear on their own submenus.

The Lotus 1-2-3 @ function reference entries in the second part are grouped according to the role they perform, as follows:

- Mathematical functions
- Scientific functions
- Statistical functions
- Financial functions
- Date and time functions
- Logical functions
- Database statistical functions
- String functions
- Special functions

Within each category, the individual @ functions are presented in alphabetical order.

Each @ function entry gives you the function name, a short description of what the function does, the syntax required by the function, and a section on how the function is used, followed by examples, special comments, and references to related commands and/or functions, if applicable.

Appendix A discusses the most important new features of Release 2.2: the Undo capability, the Allways add-in program (available to Release 2.0 users as a separate utility from Funk Software), linking, and macro libraries.

Appendix B presents an alphabetical listing of the Lotus 1-2-3 macro language commands.

Typographical Conventions

A few typographical conventions are worth noting. Consider the following key sequence, for the /Worksheet Insert command:

/WI *<C/R>* *<range>* **Return**

Here, **boldface** type indicates keys to be pressed exactly as shown. Light *italic* type indicates a step at which you must either select an alternative (as *<C/R>* to insert either a column or a row) or provide a particular value (as *<range>* to specify a range of columns or rows). Angle brackets separate such steps from each other. **Return** is the key that on some keyboards appears as Enter or the ↵ symbol. (The Lotus 1-2-3 documentation and screen messages call it Enter.)

In a list of options, boldface type marks the default selection.

Overview of Lotus 1-2-3

Lotus 1-2-3 combines spreadsheet, graphics, and database management features into a single menu-driven program. The majority of commands are issued to Lotus 1-2-3 by pressing the slash key (/) to bring up the command menu and then selecting the appropriate menu option. You can select a menu option either by typing the initial letter of the command word, or by using the cursor keys to highlight the selection and then pressing Return.

Most Lotus 1-2-3 menus are attached to submenus. Once you select a particular option from the Main Menu, you are presented with a list of new menu options that can be selected in the same way. To back up a menu level in Lotus 1-2-3, press the Esc key (universally used as the cancel key in Lotus 1-2-3). To clear the menu structure completely and return to work in the worksheet, press the Break key combination (Ctrl-Scroll Lock on most keyboards).

Not all Lotus 1-2-3 commands are selected from the command menu structure just outlined. Lotus 1-2-3 assigns commonly used commands to the ten function keys. Table I.1 shows you the commands assigned to each function key in Lotus 1-2-3. Function keys F1–F10 are also used in combination with the Alt key.

When you start up Lotus 1-2-3, you are presented with a blank worksheet arranged in columns and rows in which to enter your spreadsheet or your database information. There are 256 columns lettered A–IV (letters are doubled after Z so that the next column is AA, and so on) and there are 8192 rows numbered sequentially.

Lotus 1-2-3 accepts only two kinds of entries:

1. Labels, which must be prefaced with one of the label prefixes (see Table I.2), or begun with an alphabetical character (A–Z) or a symbol other than +, −, 0–9, @, #, or $.
2. Values, which must begin with ., + , −, the numbers 0–9, @, #, or $. Values in Lotus 1-2-3 can be either constants such as 9.7 or formulas such as +A3/B4 or @SUM(C5..C20).

Table I.1: Function-key assignments

KEY	FUNCTION
Alt-F1 (Compose)	Used to enter one of the characters in the Lotus International Character Set.
Alt-F2 (Step)	Executes macros in single-step mode.
Alt-F3 (Run)	In Release 2.2, helps you run a macro by displaying a list of range names.
Alt-F4 (Undo)	In Release 2.2, cancels the last change to the spreadsheet. Pressing it after deleting a range will recall that range. If you press **Alt-F4** again, it will delete the range again.
Alt-F5 (Learn)	In Release 2.2, records keystrokes in the record range, defined by typing **/WLR**. Pressing it again will turn recording off.
Alt-F7 (App1)	In Release 2.2 READY mode, activates any add-in program assigned to Alt-F7.
Alt-F8 (App2)	In Release 2.2 READY mode, activates any add-in program assigned to Alt-F8.
Alt-F9 (App3)	In Release 2.2 READY mode, activates any add-in program assigned to Alt-F9.
Alt-F10 (App4)	In Release 2.2 READY mode, activates any add-in program assigned to Alt-F10.
F1 (Help)	Obtains Lotus 1-2-3 on-line help.
F2 (Edit)	Used to edit the contents of the current cell.
F3 (Name)	In POINT mode, displays a line listing of range names in use. Displays full-screen view of file names when using various /File commands.
F4 (Absolute)	In POINT or EDIT mode, changes relative cell references to mixed or absolute references.
F5 (Goto)	Moves cell pointer to a specific cell.
F6 (Window)	Moves cell pointer between currently defined windows.

Table I.1: Function-key assignments (continued)

KEY	FUNCTION
F7 (Query)	Repeats previously used data query operation.
F8 (Table)	Repeats previously used data table operation.
F9 (Calc)	Recalculates formulas in worksheet.
F10 (Graph)	Displays the current graph.

Table I.2: Label prefixes

LABEL PREFIX	FUNCTION
' (apostrophe)	Left-aligned in the cell (program default unless changed).
^ (circumflex)	Centered in the cell.
" (double quote)	Right-aligned (like values) in the cell.
\ (backslash)	Repeats character typed after it across entire cell width.

Note: Use one of these label prefixes to force a value to be entered as a label, such as '1st Quarter.

The cell pointer is moved around the worksheet using various cursor keys (see Table I.3). This can only be done when the program is in READY mode (indicated by the word *READY* in the upper right corner of your screen). Once you begin making an entry in the current cell (indicated by the cell address in the upper left corner of the screen and the position of the cell pointer in the worksheet), Lotus 1-2-3 goes into either LABEL or VALUE mode, depending upon the initial character that you enter.

As you type, the label, number, or formula that you are entering is shown only on the edit line, not in the current cell. It is only when you press Return that the entry is displayed in the cell itself. If the entry is a formula, the calculated result will be displayed in the cell in the worksheet. The formula that underlies this result is shown only after the current cell address indicator.

Table I.3: Cursor-key assignments

MODE	KEY	FUNCTION
In READY or POINT mode	→	Moves cell pointer one column to right.
	←	Moves cell pointer one column to left.
	↑	Moves cell pointer up one row.
	↓	Moves cell pointer down one row.
	Home	Moves cell pointer to the first cell of the worksheet (A1 unless titles are in effect).
	End	Used with the arrow keys or the Home key. If cell pointer is in an empty cell, End moves it to the next occupied cell in the direction of the arrow. If cell pointer is in an occupied cell, End moves it to the next empty cell in the direction of the arrow. If End is used with Home, cell pointer moves to the last active cell in the worksheet.
	PgUp	Moves cell pointer up one screen.
	PgDn	Moves cell pointer down one screen.
	Tab or Ctrl-→	Moves cell pointer right one screen.
	Shift-Tab or Ctrl-←	Moves cell pointer left one screen.
In EDIT mode	→	Moves cursor one character to right.
	←	Moves cursor one character to left.
	↑	Enters contents into cell and moves cell pointer up one row.

Table I.3: Cursor-key assignments (continued)

MODE	KEY	FUNCTION
In EDIT mode (continued)	↓	Enters contents into cell and moves cell pointer down one row.
	Home	Moves cursor to first character.
	End	Moves cursor to last character.
	PgUp	Enters contents into cell and moves cell pointer up one screen.
	PgDn	Enters contents into cell and moves cell pointer down one screen.
	Tab	Moves cursor five spaces to right.
	Shift-Tab	Moves cursor five spaces to left.

As you continue to enter labels, numbers, and formulas in your spreadsheet, Lotus 1-2-3 continues to recalculate each formula in the worksheet, automatically updating the calculated results, if required. As your spreadsheet gets bigger, you will notice that it takes longer for Lotus 1-2-3 to perform this global recalculation. At such a time, you will want change the mode of recalculation from automatic to manual and force the program to recalculate your formulas only when you press F9 (Calc); see /Worksheet Global Recalculation.

To change a particular entry, you can move the cell pointer to the cell that contains it and either retype it and press Return (it will replace the original entry), or press F2 (Edit). When you press F2, the program returns the contents of the cell (the label, number, or formula) to the edit line. You can then use the cursor, Backspace, and Del keys to make the appropriate changes before pressing Return to enter the edited contents into the cell (see Table I.3).

1

The /Worksheet Menu

The /Worksheet menu contains commands that control either the entire worksheet or entire sections of it, such as entire columns or rows.

In Release 2.2, the /Worksheet Learn command has been added to help you create macros more easily.

OPTIONS

- Global
- Insert
- Delete
- Column
- Erase
- Titles
- Window
- Status
- Page
- Learn (Release 2.2 only)

/WG

The /Worksheet Global Menu

In Release 2.2, this command shows a full screen display of the current global settings, as illustrated in Figure 1.1.

KEY SEQUENCE

/WG *<option>*

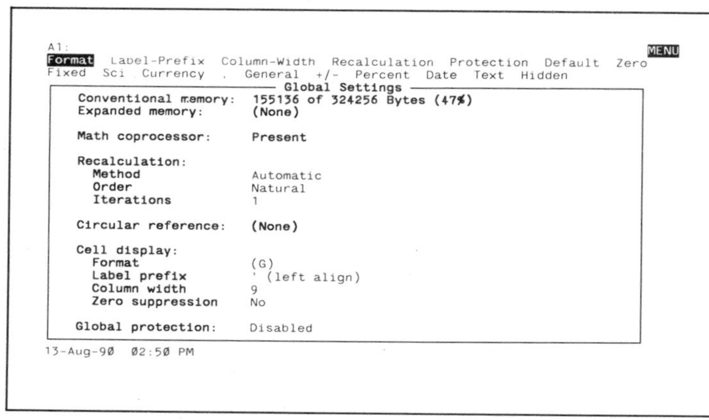

Figure 1.1: The Global settings sheet

OPTIONS

- Format
- Label-Prefix
- Column-Width
- Recalculation
- Protection
- Default
- Zero

/Worksheet Global Format

This command sets a new global display format for the worksheet. It affects all values in the worksheet not previously formatted with / Range Format.

KEY SEQUENCE

/WGF *<option>*

OPTIONS

- Fixed
- Sci
- Currency
- +/−
- Percent
- Date

- , (comma)
- **General**
- Text
- Hidden

For a discussion of the Format options, see /Range Format.

EXAMPLE

To format all of the values that you will enter or that will be calculated in a new worksheet to the Currency format, type

/WGFC

and press Return to accept the default of 2 decimal places.

SEE ALSO

/Range Format

/Worksheet Global Label-Prefix

This command changes the label default of left-justified to either right-justified or centered in the cell. It is referred to as Label-Prefix because it automatically adds either the quote (") for right justification or the circumflex (^) for centered, instead of the apostrophe ('), before any entry completed while the program is in LABEL mode.

KEY SEQUENCE

/WGL *<L/R/C>*

OPTIONS

- **Left** (')
- Right (")
- Center (^)

You will usually leave the Lotus 1-2-3 global label prefix set to the apostrophe, because only left-justified labels are displayed in adjacent blank cells to the right when they are longer than the column width. Enter **C** or **R** whenever the majority of the labels entered are to be either centered or right-justified in their cells.

NOTE

You can override the global label prefix by using the /Range Label command with either of the other two options not specified as global or by typing a different label prefix character (^ , ', or ") to change the formatting of a label display as you are entering it.

EXAMPLE

To make right justification the default for labels in a new worksheet, enter

/WGLR

SEE ALSO

/Range Label

/Worksheet Global Column-Width

This command changes the width of all of the columns in the entire worksheet (from A to IV) from the default width of 9 to a new setting of your choice.

KEY SEQUENCE

/WGC *<n>* **Return**

The column width, *n*, can be from 1 to 240. You can also press either the → or ← key to use pointing to increase or decrease the width.

NOTE

To later modify a particular column or group of columns to a different width, use the /Worksheet Column Set-Width or /Worksheet Column Column-Range Set-Width command.

SEE ALSO

/Worksheet Column Set-Width
/Worksheet Column Column-Range Set-Width

/Worksheet Global Recalculation

The /Worksheet Global Recalculation function allows you to set the method of recalculation to Manual or back to Automatic, change the number of Iterations used each time the worksheet is recalculated, or change the order of recalculation to Columnwise, Rowwise, or back to Natural.

KEY SEQUENCE

/WGC <*n*> **Return**

OPTIONS

- **Natural**: seldom changed
- Columnwise
- Rowwise
- **Automatic**
- Manual: When the default setting of Automatic is changed to Manual, formulas are recalculated only when you press F9 (Calc).
- Iteration: 1 to 50 (default: 1)

EXAMPLES

To set recalculation to Manual, merely type **/WGRM** from anywhere in the worksheet. To set it back to Automatic, type **/WGRA**.

To change the number of iterations, type **/WGRI** and the number you wish to set. Then press Return. When you want to reset the number of iterations back to 1, reissue the command and enter **1** before pressing Return.

SEE ALSO

/Worksheet Status

/Worksheet Global Protection Enable

This command protects the entire worksheet from further revisions of any kind.

KEY SEQUENCE

/WGPE

Once global protection has been enabled, no one can edit, delete, reformat, or in any way change the contents of the cells entered when creating the spreadsheet or add new entries in other areas. Any attempt to add new entries or edit existing ones results in the program going into ERROR mode. The user also receives the error message *Protected cell.* Lotus 1-2-3 indicates that protection has been enabled by adding the abbreviation PR before the display of the cell's literal contents on the first line of the Control Panel.

Undoing /Worksheet Global Protection Enable

If you need to make revisions to part of a spreadsheet that has been globally protected, use the /Worksheet Global Protection Disable command (**/WGPD**) to lift the protection. After making any required changes, globally protect the worksheet once again with /WGPE.

After you enable global protection, you can then unprotect particular input cells by using the /Range Unprot command.

SEE ALSO

/Range Prot
/Range Unprot

/Worksheet Global Default

This command is used to configure the default printer interface and settings, to set the Currency, Date, and Time formats, to change the display of the on-screen clock/calendar, and to modify access to the help files.

In Release 2.2, this command displays a full screen with all of the current default settings. Figure 1.2 shows this screen. The /Worksheet Global Default Other menu in this release also allows you to configure the new Undo feature, to run a macro automatically each time you retrieve a document, and to set up Add-in programs.

To make your settings permanent, you must save any changes you make by using the Update option.

```
A1:                                                                    MENU
Printer  Directory  Status  Update  Other  Autoexec  Quit
Specify printer interface and default settings
                              Default Settings
 Printer:                                    Directory: C:\LOTUS\DATA
   Interface        Parallel 1
   Auto linefeed    No                       Autoexecute macros: Yes
   Margins
     Left 4   Right 76   Top 2   Bottom 2    International:
   Page length      66                         Punctuation          A
   Wait             No                           Decimal            Period
   Setup string                                  Argument           Comma
   Name             HP 2686 LaserJet Se...       Thousands          Comma
                                               Currency             Prefix: $
 Add-In:                                       Date format (D4)     A (MM/DD/YY)
   1                                           Time format (D8)     A (HH:MM:SS)
   2                                           Negative             Parentheses
   3
   4                                         Help access method:  Removable
   5                                         Clock display:       Standard
   6                                         Undo:                Enabled
   7                                         Beep:                Yes
   8
21-Aug-90  09:41 PM
```

Figure 1.2: The Default settings sheet

KEY SEQUENCE

/WGD *<option>*

OPTIONS

- Printer: Type of interface; auto-linefeed (Y or N); margins; page length; wait (Y or N); setup string; select new printer by name; quit.
- Directory: Sets default drive and directory for saving and retrieving data files.
- Status: Displays current defaults.
- Update: Saves changes made to default settings.
- Other: See following section.
- Autoexec: Specifies whether you want an autoexec macro (labeled with 10) to be executed automatically on startup.
- Quit: Returns to /Worksheet Global menu.

Worksheet Global Default Other

This menu is used to modify several of Lotus 1-2-3's default settings. It allows you to change general display formats, control the new Undo feature, and configure add-ins. You can also specify what information appears on the last line of the screen.

To save any new settings, select the /Worksheet Global Default Update command after making your changes.

KEY SEQUENCE

/WGDO *<option>*

OPTIONS

- International: allows you to change punctuation, currency symbols, date and time formats, and negative symbols.
- Help: lets you choose how Lotus 1-2-3 treats the help file. If you choose Instant, 1-2-3 will keep the help file open at all times and help will come up faster. If you remove the help disk with this option on, you risk a system failure. If you choose Removable, this file will remain closed when not in use.
- Clock: sets the display at the bottom of the screen as Standard (DD-MMM-YY and HH:MM(AM/PM)), International (as set by /Worksheet Global Default Other International), Filename, or None.
- Undo: turns the Undo feature on or off.
- Beep: determines whether 1-2-3 sounds beep (computer bell) on errors and {BEEP} macro commands.
- Add-In: sets and attaches, or cancels and detaches, an add-in program (specified by number, 1–8) to be run whenever you start Lotus 1-2-3.

/Worksheet Global Zero

This command can suppress the display of all zero values throughout the worksheet or replace them with a label you provide.

/WGZN

Undoing /Worksheet Global Zero

To redisplay zeros in the worksheet, enter **/WGZY**.

Replacing Zeros with a Label

Release 2.2 allows you to replace all zeros in your spreadsheet with a label, such as "-0-". Enter **/WGZL** and then type the label you want in all zero cells.

The /Worksheet Insert Command

This command inserts entire new columns or rows in the worksheet.

KEY SEQUENCE

/WI *<C/R>* *<range>* **Return**

Use the **C** option to add a new *column* or range of columns from the current cell pointer's position; use the **R** option to add a new *row* or range of rows. The program will supply the current cell address as the default. To add more than a single new column (or row), indicate the *range* by highlighting a group of adjacent columns (or rows) with pointing or by typing in the cell addresses.

As soon as you press Return after indicating the range with either command, the program inserts the blank column(s) or row(s) at the cell pointer's position. A row is inserted above the specified row range; a column is inserted to the left of the specified column range. The data located in cells displaced by the insertion of new columns or rows is automatically moved to new locations. All of the cell references in any formulas are adjusted to reflect the new addresses.

If you wish to add blank cells in only a portion of a column or a row, you must use the /Move command.

EXAMPLE

To insert two new rows above row 2 in a worksheet, position the cell pointer in any column of row 2, type

/WIR

and move the cell pointer to highlight down to row 4 before pressing Return.

SEE ALSO

/Move

The /Worksheet Delete Command

This command deletes entire columns or rows from the worksheet.

KEY SEQUENCE

/WD *<C/R>* *<range>* **Return**

Use the **C** option to delete a *column* or range of columns from the current cell pointer's position; use the **R** option to delete a *row* or range of rows. The program will supply the current cell address as the default (though it takes into consideration only the column letter). To delete more than a single new column (or row), you can then indicate a *range* by highlighting a group of adjacent columns (or rows) with pointing or by typing in cell addresses.

As soon as you press Return after indicating the range with either command, the program deletes all of the data contained in the column(s) or row(s) from the cell pointer's position. The data located outside the column(s) or row(s) is automatically moved to new locations. All of the cell references in any formulas are adjusted to reflect the new addresses.

NOTE

If any of the cell references in the remaining formulas refer to data that was deleted, zeros, error values, or circular references may suddenly appear in some of them. Before using the /Worksheet Delete commands, you should always exercise the precaution of first saving the worksheet if it has never been saved before.

If you wish to delete data in only a portion of a column or row, you must use the /Range Erase command.

EXAMPLE

To delete the data in columns B and C in a worksheet, position the cell pointer in any row of column B, type

/WDC

and move the cell pointer right to highlight column C before pressing Return.

SEE ALSO

/Range Erase

/WC

The /Worksheet Column Command

This command allows you to change the width of worksheet columns.

KEY SEQUENCE

/WC *<option>*

OPTIONS

- Set-Width
- Reset-Width
- Hide
- Display
- Column-Range (Release 2.2 only)

/Worksheet Column Set-Width

KEY SEQUENCE

After positioning the cell pointer anywhere in the column, type

/WCS *<n>* **Return**

to set a width for only that particular column. The default is 9 characters. The new column width, *n*, can be 1 to 240 characters.

/Worksheet Column Reset-Width

KEY SEQUENCE

After placing the pointer anywhere in the column, press

/WCR

to change the column width back to the global default for any columns you have previously modified with the /Worksheet Column Set-Width or /Worksheet Column Column-Range Set-Width commands.

/Worksheet Column Hide

This option makes the display of the specified column of the worksheet invisible.

KEY SEQUENCE

Position the pointer anywhere in the column and give the command

/WCH <*range*> **Return**

The letter of the hidden column is no longer shown in the border area. You can hide a range of columns by typing the address of the range or by pointing to the cells.

/Worksheet Column Display

This option redisplays any column masked by the use of the Hide option.

KEY SEQUENCE

/WCD <*range*> **Return**

When you use this option, Lotus 1-2-3 displays an asterisk after the letter of all hidden columns in the border area. To unhide a column, first display it; then move the pointer to one of its cells and press Return.

/Worksheet Column Column-Range (Release 2.2 only)

This option changes the width of a range of columns.

KEY SEQUENCE

Position the pointer anywhere in the range of columns and give the command

/WCC *<S/R>* *<range>* **Return**

OPTION

- Set-Width: Sets the width of that group of columns. The default is 9 characters. The new column width can be 1 to 240 characters.
- Reset-Width: Changes the width of columns in the range back to the global default. This is used to change columns you have previously modified with /Worksheet Column Set-Width or /Worksheet Column Column-Range Set-Width commands.

SEE ALSO

/Worksheet Global Column-Width
/Range Format Hide

/WE

The /Worksheet Erase Command

The /Worksheet Erase command clears the current worksheet file loaded into Lotus 1-2-3 from the computer's memory.

KEY SEQUENCE

/WE *<Y/N>*

To clear the current worksheet to begin work on a new spreadsheet, choose **Y** for yes. This command is not required if all you want to do is load another worksheet file into memory. The /File Retrieve command automatically clears the current worksheet before loading the new file you indicate. Always make sure that you have saved the worksheet in memory before you use this command.

SEE ALSO

/File Retrieve

/WT

The /Worksheet Titles Command

This command locks the columns to the left or rows above the cell pointer's current position in place on the display screen.

KEY SEQUENCE

/WT

OPTIONS

- Both
- Horizontal
- Vertical
- Clear

/Worksheet Titles Horizontal

This option makes titles out of the rows that are located above the cell pointer's position when you issue the command.

KEY SEQUENCE

After locating the cell pointer anywhere in the row right below the rows you wish to include in the titles area, type

/WTH

/Worksheet Titles Vertical

This option makes titles out of the columns immediately to the left of the cell pointer's position when you issue the command.

KEY SEQUENCE

After locating the cell pointer in the column immediately to the right of the column (or columns) you wish to include in the titles area, type

/WTV

/Worksheet Titles Both

This option designates both the columns to the left and the rows above the cell pointer's current position (that is, the current cell) as titles in the spreadsheet.

KEY SEQUENCE

After locating the cell pointer in a cell directly below the row (or rows) as well as directly to the right of the column (or columns) to be included, enter

/WTB

After you issue the command, you will be unable to move the pointer either up or left into the newly created titles area.

/Worksheet Titles Clear

This option clears any titles that have been created in the full-screen display or in the window in which the cell pointer is located.

KEY SEQUENCE

/WTC

NOTE

When you use the /Worksheet Titles commands after you have split the display with one of the /Worksheet Window options, the titles affect only the window that contains the cell pointer at the time you issue the Titles command. This allows you to set up different titles areas in each window you have created.

SEE ALSO

/Worksheet Window

The /Worksheet Window Command

This command splits the Lotus 1-2-3 worksheet display area into separate viewing areas along either a horizontal or a vertical axis of your choice, effectively creating two windows on the data contained in a single spreadsheet.

KEY SEQUENCE

/WW *<option>*

OPTIONS

- Horizontal
- Vertical
- Sync
- Unsync
- Clear

/Worksheet Window Horizontal

This command is used to split the worksheet display at a specific row (horizontal windowing).

KEY SEQUENCE

/WWH

/Worksheet Window Vertical

This command is used to split the worksheet display at a specific column (vertical windowing).

KEY SEQUENCE

/WWV

NOTE

To move the cell pointer back and forth between the windows you create with these commands, press the Window key (F6).

/Worksheet Windows Unsync

When you use the Horizontal window option, all horizontal scrolling with the Tab or Backtab keys is synchronized automatically in horizontal windows unless you use the /Worksheet Windows Unsync command. When you use the Vertical window option, all vertical scrolling with the PgDn or PgUp keys is synchronized automatically in vertical windows unless you use the /Worksheet Windows Unsync command.

KEY SEQUENCE

/WWU

/Worksheet Windows Sync

Use this command to return to synchronized scrolling.

KEY SEQUENCE

/WWS

/Worksheet Windows Clear

Use this command to clear either horizontal or vertical windows and return to a single spreadsheet display.

KEY SEQUENCE

/WWC

SEE ALSO

/Worksheet Titles

/WS

The /Worksheet Status Command

This command displays information on the amount of conventional memory, the method and order of recalculation, the global cell display for values and labels, the global column-width setting, and the status of global protection. It also includes additional information: statistics for the amount of expanded memory, presence of a math coprocessor, circular references in the spreadsheet, the number of iterations set, and the status of zero suppression.

Release 2.2 users can also see this display by typing **/WG**; it is illustrated under the /Worksheet Global heading in this chapter as Figure 1.1.

KEY SEQUENCE

/WS

SEE ALSO

/Worksheet Global

/WP

The /Worksheet Page Command

This command is used to place a page break command at a particular row in the spreadsheet before printing it.

KEY SEQUENCE

After positioning the cell pointer in the row containing the first line of data you want to be printed on a new page, and in the leftmost column of the print range, enter

/WP

Lotus 1-2-3 will insert a new row at the current cell's position. The double colon (::) represents the page break symbol. The page break will not occur in the report unless the page break symbol is located in the leftmost cell of the designated print range.

Undoing the /Worksheet Page Command

To delete a page break entered with the /WP command, move the cell pointer to the row containing the page break symbol and delete the entire row by using the /Worksheet Delete Row command—type **/WDR** and press Return.

SEE ALSO

/Worksheet Delete
/Print

/WL

2.2

The /Worksheet Learn Command

This command is used to set up a *Learn Range*, an area of the spreadsheet where you can create macros as you execute the commands. Lotus 1-2-3 now "learns" your macros as you type them. Once you have defined one or more rows in a column as your Learn Range, press Alt-F5 to record your keystrokes in that range. Enter the keystrokes and press Alt-F5 when you are done. The keystrokes you typed will be in the first empty cell(s) of your Learn Range.

KEY SEQUENCE

Position the pointer to the first cell you want in your Learn Range and enter

/WLR <*range*> **Return**

The range you specify should be in one column. 1-2-3 will let you record only as many macros as you have lines in your Learn Range. Type **/WLC** to cancel the learn range you defined with /WLR, and type **/WLE** to erase it. Use **/WLR** again if you need to redefine the range.

OPTIONS

- Range: specifies a range for storing Learn macros.
- Cancel: Cancels the Learn Range.
- Erase: Erases all information in the Learn Range.

2

The /Range Menu

The /Range menu contains commands that control just a partial section of the worksheet, defined by cell addresses.

OPTIONS

- Format
- Label
- Erase
- Name
- Justify
- Prot
- Unprot
- Input
- Value
- Trans
- Search

/RF

The /Range Format Command

This command sets a new display format for a range of values that you designate. Regardless of the display formats available from this menu, Lotus 1-2-3 stores each numerical value to a precision of 15 decimal places. Changing the display format in the worksheet itself does not affect this precision.

KEY SEQUENCE

/RF *<option>* *<n>* **Return** *<range>* **Return**

Choose the desired format from the menu *options* that appear. If necessary, enter the number of decimal places (*n*) from 1 to 15 (default: 2). Then, designate the *range* of cells to be formatted either by typing in their cell addresses or by using pointing.

OPTIONS

- Fixed
- Sci
- Currency
- , (comma)
- **General**
- +/−
- Percent
- Date
- Text
- Hidden
- Reset

The Fixed Format

The Fixed format allows you to choose the number of decimal points to be displayed in values in the range.

KEY SEQUENCE

/RFF *<n>* **Return** *<range>* **Return**

The Sci Format

The Sci format displays all values in exponential notation. You can specify the number of decimal places to be displayed before the exponent.

KEY SEQUENCE

/RFS *<n>* **Return** *<range>* **Return**

The Currency Format

The Currency format displays all values in a dollar-and-cents format in which a dollar sign precedes numbers, commas separate thousands, and negative numbers are in parentheses.

KEY SEQUENCE

/RFC *<n>* **Return** *<range>* **Return**

NOTE

You can change the currency symbol used in this format as well as the thousands and decimal-point delimiters by using the /Worksheet Global Default Other International command (**/WGDOI**). Any changes made to the Punctuation and/or Currency options that appear after you use this command are picked up when you choose the Currency format.

The , (Comma) Format

The , (comma) format displays values in the same way as the Currency format, except that it does not preface the value with a dollar sign.

KEY SEQUENCE

/RF, *<n>* **Return** *<range>* **Return**

NOTE

Any changes made with the /Worksheet Global Default Other International command (**/WGDOI**) are also reflected in the , (comma) format.

The General Format

The General format is the Lotus 1-2-3 global default at start-up. You choose this format to change the global format back to General after you use one of the other options listed on the menu. The number of decimal places displayed before the exponent is always 2 when the General format is in effect.

KEY SEQUENCE

/RFG *<n>* **Return** *<range>* **Return**

The +/− Format

The +/− format is referred to as a horizontal bar graph format. It converts all values into a corresponding number of pluses (positive values) or minuses (negative values). A zero value is displayed as a decimal point.

KEY SEQUENCE

/RF+ *<range>* **Return**

The Percent Format

The Percent format displays the values in the range as percentages by multiplying the value by 100 and adding a trailing percent sign (%).

KEY SEQUENCE

/RFP *<n>* **Return** *<range>* **Return**

NOTE

Any changes made to the International Punctuation command are also reflected in this format.

The Date Format

The Date format displays all values in the range in one of the date formats you specify after selecting this command.

KEY SEQUENCE

/RFD *<option>* *<range>* **Return**

OPTIONS

- 1 (DD-MMM-YY)
- 2 (DD-MMM)
- 3 (MMM-YY)
- 4 (Long Intn'l): default: MM/DD/YY

- 5 (Short Intn'l): default: MM/DD
- Time

The Time Option

OPTIONS

- 1 (HH:MM:SS AM/PM)
- 2 (HH:MM AM/PM)
- 3 (Long Intn'l): HH:MM:SS, 24-hour clock
- 4 (Short Intn'l):HH:MM, 24-hour clock

NOTE

You can modify the punctuation and style of these formats by using the International Date and Time menus (**/WGDO**).

The Text Format

The Text format displays all formulas used in the range in place of their calculated values. Where literal values have been used, the program uses the General display.

KEY SEQUENCE

/RFT *<range>* **Return**

The Hidden Format

The Hidden format suppresses the display of all cells in the range. Their contents are displayed only on the first line of the Control Panel when the cell pointer makes the individual cell current. Because only cell contents, not calculated values, are displayed on the Control Panel line, you cannot see their calculated values; you can see only the formulas.

KEY SEQUENCE

/RFH *<range>* **Return**

Reset

The Reset command returns the designated range of cells to their original global format.

KEY SEQUENCE

/RFR *<range>* **Return**

EXAMPLE

To format a range of values in the cell range E32..F45 to the Currency format, take the following steps:

1. Move the cell pointer to cell E32 and type **/RFC**.
2. Press Return to accept two decimal places.
3. Use pointing to highlight the range E32..F45 and press Return again.

SEE ALSO

/Worksheet Global Format

/RL

The /Range Label Command

This command changes the justification of labels in a designated range. Most often, this involves changing the labels in the range from the default of left-justified to either centered or right-justified. Whatever new option is chosen overrides the global label prefix in effect or the /Range Label option last used to format the labels in the range.

KEY SEQUENCE

/RL *<L/R/C>* *<range>* **Return**

Type either **L** for left-justified, **R** for right-justified, or **C** for centered.

EXAMPLE

To right-align a range of labels in the cell range A3..D3, take the following steps:

1. Move the cell pointer to cell A3 and type **/RLR**.
2. Press the → key to highlight the range A3..D3 and press Return to reformat the labels.

SEE ALSO

/Worksheet Global Label-Prefix

/RE

The /Range Erase Command

This command deletes the contents of the current cell or a range of cells, beginning with the current cell. Using the /Range Erase command is the only way to delete a cell's contents without replacing them with something else.

KEY SEQUENCE

After positioning the cell pointer in the cell to be deleted or at the beginning of the range of cells to be deleted, type

/RE *<range>* **Return**

EXAMPLE

To erase the cell range T2..U4, take the following steps:

1. Move the cell pointer to T2 and type **/RE**.
2. Use the arrow keys to highlight the range T2..U4 and press Return.

Undoing /Range Erase

NOTES

With the new Undo feature in Release 2.2, you can now retrieve a range which you mistakenly deleted. Simply press **Alt-F5** to cancel the last change you made. This key will undo only those changes made since you were last in the READY mode. See Appendix A for more information on the Undo feature.

The use of the /Range Erase command differs from that of the /Worksheet Delete Column and Row commands. Though these /Worksheet Delete commands also erase any cell entries located in the columns or rows specified, they do not work on a partial column or row of data. The /Range Erase command provides the only method in Lotus 1-2-3 for deleting partial columns and rows.

SEE ALSO

/Worksheet Delete
/Worksheet Erase

/RN

The /Range Name Command

The /Range Name command assigns the name you enter to any valid cell range in the spreadsheet. The range name is then saved with the spreadsheet and can be used in place of cell addresses in commands that require cell ranges as inputs. If you name individual cells (the smallest Lotus 1-2-3 range), you can use their names in formulas and as arguments of functions that allow only single values. You can also move the cell pointer directly to the beginning of a named range by pressing F5 (Goto) followed by F3 (Name) and then highlighting the range name and pressing Return.

KEY SEQUENCE

/RN *<option>*

OPTIONS

- Create
- Delete
- Labels
- Reset
- Table

/Range Name Create

This command lets you name ranges in the spreadsheet.

KEY SEQUENCE

/RNC <*name*> **Return** <*range*> **Return**

The program prompts you for the range name and the cell addresses of the range. The range *name* can be up to 15 characters long. It should not begin with any valid cell address or mathematical operator. You can include spaces between the words, though it is common practice to use underlines.

The *range* can be any valid Lotus 1-2-3 cell range. The program will suggest the current cell address as the range (as in A1..A1). You can enter the location of the range to be named either by typing in the addresses of its first and last cells or by pointing.

NOTES

Lotus 1-2-3 allows you to give more than one name to the same cell range. Different range names can be given to overlapping cell ranges with this command. However, if you assign the same name to two different cell ranges, Lotus 1-2-3 will recognize only the last-named range by that name.

As soon as you assign a range name to a cell range with this command, the range name appears in the literal contents of all formulas that contain references to it.

Whenever you type **/RNC** to name a new range, Lotus 1-2-3 displays an alphabetical listing of all range names currently in use. If you intend to use an assigned name for a different range in the spreadsheet, you can use the → and ← keys to move the highlight to the name and select it by pressing Return.

EXAMPLE

To assign the range name ACCT_BAL to the cell range F50..G51, take the following steps:

1. Type **/RNC**.
2. Enter **ACCT_BAL** as the range name and press Return.
3. Indicate the range of cells by entering F50..G51 and press Return.

/Range Name Labels

This command allows you to use labels already entered in the spreadsheet as names for ranges located in adjacent cell ranges.

KEY SEQUENCE

After locating the cell pointer in the cell that contains the label you wish to assign as the range name, type

/RNL <*option*> **Return** <*range*> **Return**

where you type the first letter of the *option* or highlight it. The program prompts you for the cell *range* containing all of the labels you wish to use as range names. You can indicate this cell range by typing in the cell addresses or by pointing to them. If you are using only the label in the current cell, simply press Return.

OPTIONS

- Right: names cell ranges in the columns directly to the right of the labels.
- Down: names cell ranges in the rows directly beneath the labels.
- Left: names cell ranges in the columns directly to the left of the labels.
- Up: names cell ranges in the rows directly above the labels.

NOTE

Lotus 1-2-3 macros are defined by giving the first cell that contains the macro keystrokes and commands a special range name that consists of a single letter (A–Z) preceded by a \. These range names can be assigned by using either the /Range Name Create or Labels command. If you use the /Range Name Labels command, place the macro name (such as \E) in the cell immediately to the left of the first cell containing macro commands and select the Right option.

/Range Name Delete

Use this command to delete an individual range name in use.

KEY SEQUENCE

/RND *<name>* **Return**

Lotus 1-2-3 will display an alphabetical listing of the range names you have already created. Use the → key to move the highlight to it and press Return.

NOTE

As soon as you delete range names, all formulas that contain references to their assigned ranges revert back to cell addressing. Instead of the range name being displayed in the literal contents, you will then see only the cell addresses.

/Range Names Reset

Use this command to delete all the range names you have created at once.

KEY SEQUENCE

/RNR **Return**

NOTE

As soon as you delete range names, all formulas that contain references to their assigned ranges revert back to cell addressing. Instead of the range name being displayed in the literal contents, you will then see only the cell addresses.

/Range Name Table

This command allows you to create a table of all range names currently in use.

KEY SEQUENCE

/RNT *<range>* **Return**

This command creates a two-column table in the spreadsheet in the cell *range* you indicate. The first column of this table contains an alphabetical listing of the range names. The second column indicates their present location by cell addresses.

NOTES

A range table overwrites any existing data that is located in the range indicated. You need to indicate only the beginning cell address of the range for locating the table. Lotus 1-2-3 will fill in the table from that point, using subsequent cells as needed.

The range-name table created with this command is static. As you continue to work in the spreadsheet and assign new range names, you will need to reissue the /Range Name Table command if you wish to keep the table current.

/RJ

The /Range Justify Command

This command reformats long label entries so that they fit within the narrower justify range indicated.

KEY SEQUENCE

After positioning the cell pointer in the cell where you want the label to be, type

/RJ *<range>* **Return**

You can indicate the extent of the range where you want the label to appear by pointing to or typing the cell addresses. After you press Return, the text will be reformatted to stay within this range, using new rows as required to display all of the labels.

You can also use this command to combine separate labels entered into vertically adjacent cells. To combine an entry, position the cell pointer in the first cell of the range and then widen the cell to display all of the combined labels. Type **/RJ** and give the current cell as the justify range by pressing Return. The program will then display in the first cell all of the labels in the adjacent cells. If there is insufficient room, not all of the labels will be combined.

/RP

The /Range Prot Command

This command protects a particular range of cells in the worksheet from any further modifications when global protection is not in effect.

KEY SEQUENCE

After moving the cell pointer to the beginning of the range, type

/RP *<range>* **Return**

NOTE

Once a range has been protected, no one can edit, delete, reformat, or in any way change the contents of the cells entered within its boundaries. Also note that protected ranges cannot be copied or moved to new places in the worksheet.

EXAMPLE

To protect the cell range A1..T45 from further changes, type **/RP**, enter A1..T45 as the range to protect, and press Return.

SEE ALSO

/Worksheet Global Protection
/Range Unprot

/RU

The /Range Unprot Command

This command removes the protection status from those ranges that have been previously protected with either the /Worksheet Global Protection Enable or the /Range Prot command.

KEY SEQUENCE

/RU *<range>* **Return**

NOTES

Use the /Range Unprot command to allow entry in input cells after setting up global protection throughout the worksheet. It can also be coupled with the /Range Input command to restrict the cell pointer to only those cells that have been unprotected with this command.

All data in ranges that are unprotected in a worksheet with global protection in effect is displayed in high intensity to set it off from the rest of the protected data. Whenever a cell within this range is current, it also displays the code U before its literal contents on the first line of the Control Panel.

EXAMPLE

To unprotect the cell range B1..D17, type **/RU**, enter B1..D17 as the range to unprotect, and press Return.

SEE ALSO

/Worksheet Global Protection Enable
/Range Input
/Range Prot

/RI

The /Range Input Command

This command restricts the cell pointer to only those cells that have been unprotected (with the /Range Unprot command) to allow new data input or revisions to take place.

KEY SEQUENCE

/RI *<range>* **Return**

NOTE

This command stays in effect only until the operator presses the Esc key. After executing the command, the cell pointer can move only to the range or ranges specified. Once the command has been executed, the following conditions are in effect:

- The Home key takes the pointer directly to the first input cell in the range instead of to cell A1 (unless A1 has been designated as the first input cell).
- The End key takes the pointer to the last input cell in the range.
- The Lotus 1-2-3 command menu is deactivated and cannot be accessed until you press Esc or Return in READY mode.
- The only function keys that are operative during its execution are F1 (Help), F2 (Edit), F9 (Calc), Alt-F1 (Compose), Alt-F2 (Step), Alt-F4 (Undo), and Alt-F5 (Learn).

SEE ALSO

/Worksheet Global Protection Enable
/Range Unprot

/RV

The /Range Value Command

The /Range Value command converts a range of formulas in a worksheet to their currently calculated values.

KEY SEQUENCE

/RV *<source range>* **Return**
<destination range> **Return**

Like the /Copy command, the /Range Value command prompts you first for the *source range* (to copy FROM) and then for the *destination range* (to copy TO). If you do not want to copy the range to a new location in the worksheet, you simply indicate the same range of cells in response to both the FROM and TO prompts.

NOTE

Copying the range to a new location allows you to maintain two copies of the same formulas: the original, which is still subject to further what-if analysis, and a new range in which the formulas are calculated and converted to their present numeric values.

EXAMPLE

To convert the calculated values in the cell range C3..D4 to constant values, take the following steps:

1. Type **/RV**, enter C3..D4 as the source range to copy FROM, and press Return.
2. Enter C3..D4 a second time as the destination range to copy TO and press Return.

SEE ALSO

/File Xtract

/RT

The /Range Trans Command

This command is used to copy and simultaneously transpose data that has been entered down columns in the source range so it is arranged across rows when copied to the destination range, or, vice versa, to transpose data that runs across rows so that it runs down columns.

The transposition will not be completely successful if the data in the source range includes formulas that use cell references. These become skewed in the copy and usually result in ERR values. To avoid this, you can use the /Range Value command to convert all formulas to their calculated values before issuing the /Range Trans command.

KEY SEQUENCE

/RT *<source range>* **Return**
<destination range> **Return**

Indicate the extent of the *source range* in response to the copy FROM prompt either by pointing or by using cell addresses, and press Return. When you indicate the source range for columns, be sure that the order given is from top to bottom; for rows, the copy of the data will be displayed down the column of the destination range in the same order as it was entered from left to right across the row in the source range. Then indicate the first cell of the *destination range*, and press Return again. For columns, the copy of the data will be displayed from left to right across the row of the destination range in the same order as it was entered down the column in the source range; for rows, from left to right.

Use this new command to search for strings or numbers in your worksheet and, if you wish, replace them with other strings or numbers.

KEY SEQUENCE

/RS *<range>* **Return** *<F/S/B>* *<F/R>* *<options>*

After you select a range to search, indicate whether you are searching for Formulas, Labels, or Both formulas and labels. Next, you choose whether to simply Find the text or number or to Replace it with something else after it is found.

If Lotus 1-2-3 cannot find what you are searching for, you will get an error message at this point. Otherwise, if you've chosen Find, you will then be prompted to either find the Next item or Quit. If you've chosen Replace, your options after a successful search are to Replace that occurrence of the item, replace All occurrences, find the Next occurrence but not replace the current one, or Quit.

3

The /Copy and /Move Commands

The /Copy command makes a copy of the data included in the source range (copy FROM) in the destination range (copy TO). The /Move command is used to move cell ranges from one area of the worksheet to another.

/C
The /Copy Command

KEY SEQUENCE

/C *<source range>* **Return**
<destination range> **Return**

Enter the *source range* of cells to be copied in response to the prompt *Enter range to copy FROM:*. Enter the *destination range* where the cell range is to be copied in response to the prompt *Enter range to copy TO:*.

The /Copy command allows you to make three types of copies in the worksheet: one to many, one to one, and many to many.

The One-to-Many Copy

KEY SEQUENCE

/C *<source cell>* **Return**
<destination range> **Return**

In the one-to-many copy, the *source* range is a single *cell* entered by cell address or range name. You can indicate a cell address by typing in the address or by pointing. The *destination range* is made up of a block of multiple cells. These, too, can be indicated by entering cell addresses or by pointing. If you are using pointing, remember to anchor the range by typing a period.

The one-to-many copy is most commonly used for copying a single formula to other cells. You must take into consideration relative versus mixed or absolute cell addressing when you create the original formula to be copied. The copy can be done in one or two dimensions, as illustrated in Figure 3.1, which shows three examples of the one-to-many copy.

The One-to-One Copy

KEY SEQUENCE

/C *<source cell>* **Return** *<destination cell>* **Return**

The one-to-one copy differs from the one-to-many copy only in that the *source* range and *destination* range are both single *cells*. This type of copy is used most often to copy a spreadsheet title or heading from one area of the worksheet to another.

However, when you need to bring forward the contents of one cell to a new area of the worksheet and you want the copy to remain dynamically linked to its source, do not use the /Copy command. In such cases, create a formula in the new cell, preceding the source cell's address with a plus sign. For instance, to bring forward the contents of cell A1 to AB20, locate the pointer in AB20 and enter the formula **+A1**. That way, any updating done in A1 will also be done in AB20.

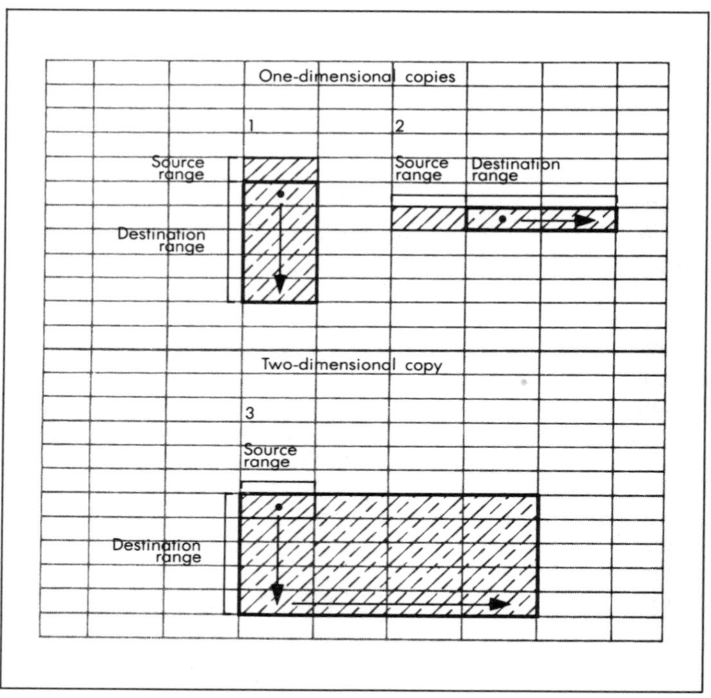

Figure 3.1: The one-to-many copy in the worksheet

The Many-to-Many Copy

KEY SEQUENCES

/C *<source range>* **Return**
<destination range> **Return**

Use the many-to-many copy when you wish to bring forward a range of cell entries, which may include any combination of labels, literal values, and formulas. In this kind of copy, the *source range* of cells must be arranged in a contiguous block. When entering the source range, you can designate it either by cell addresses or by range name. When designating cell addresses, you can type in the cell addresses or use the pointing method. If you use pointing, type a period to anchor the range.

After designating the extent of the source, indicate the location of the *destination range* by designating only its first cell (the one in the upper-left corner of the range). Lotus 1-2-3 will make the copy from this point on, filling in the rest of the copied cells as necessary. This kind of copy is illustrated in Figure 3.2.

Relative versus Absolute Cell References in Copied Formulas

When copying labels and values, Lotus 1-2-3 makes an exact copy. However, when copying formulas that contain relative cell references, it makes a relative copy whereby all cell addresses are automatically adjusted, reflecting the direction of the copy.

You can override the relative addressing default when you copy formulas: you can make all or part of the formula copy absolute. Absolute cell references in a formula are not changed in the copies made of them.

Lotus 1-2-3 uses the $ (dollar sign) as the symbol for denoting an absolute cell reference. Placing the $ before the column letter (as in $A3) prevents the column reference from being adjusted in the copies made of the formula. Placing the $ before the row number (as in A$3) prevents the row reference from being adjusted in the copies

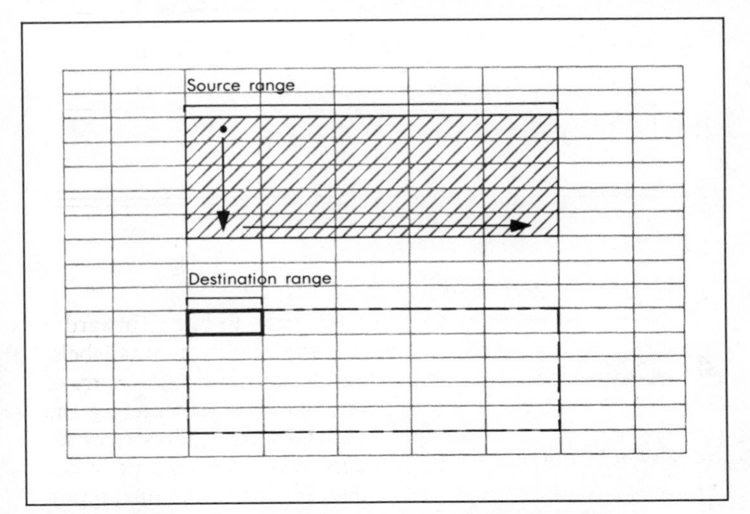

Figure 3.2: The many-to-many copy in the worksheet

made of the formula. Placing dollar signs before both the column letter and row number (as in A3) prevents adjustment of either reference in the copies made of the formula.

EXAMPLE

To copy a formula entered in cell G4 to cell range G5..G10, take the following steps:

1. Move the cell pointer to cell G4, type **/C** and press Return.
2. Type a period to anchor the cell range.
3. Press the ↓ key until the cell range G4..G10 is highlighted and press Return to make the copy.

NOTES

You can use F4 (Absolute) to place dollar signs before a cell reference in a formula to be copied when indicating the cell reference by pointing. You can also use this function key when editing a formula's contents with F2 (Edit). Pressing F4 in sequence produces different combinations of relative and absolute references, as follows:

- First time pressed produces completely absolute reference, as in B2.
- Second time pressed produces mixed reference, as in B$2.
- Third time pressed produces mixed reference, as in $B2.
- Fourth time pressed returns to completely relative reference, as in B2.

The /Move Command

KEY SEQUENCE

/M *<source range>* **Return**
<destination range> **Return**

Enter the *source range* to be moved in response to the prompt *Enter range to move FROM:*. Enter the *destination range* in response to the prompt *Enter range to move TO:*.

When indicating the source range, designate it by cell addresses or by range name. When designating cell addresses, you can either type in the cell addresses or use pointing. If you use the pointing method, type a period to anchor the range before you extend it with the appropriate arrow keys.

When indicating the destination range, you need to designate the position of only the first cell (the one in the upper-left corner of the range). Lotus 1-2-3 fills in the rest of the cells included in the range as necessary.

NOTE

Formulas that contain references to cells in the range that has been relocated with the /Move command are automatically adjusted to reflect the cells' new position in the worksheet.

EXAMPLES

To move the cell range E6..H17 to a new area beginning at cell AA10, take the following steps:

1. Type **/M**, enter E6..H17 as the source range (to move FROM), and press Return.
2. Move the cell pointer to cell AA10 or enter AA10 as the destination range (to move TO), and press Return.

If you had given the range name Data−table to the cell range E6..H17 (see /Range Name Create), you could accomplish this move as follows:

1. Move the cell pointer to the cell AA10 (the beginning of the destination cell range where you want the cell range to be copied).
2. Type **/M**, enter Data−table as the source range (to move FROM) by typing it in or pressing F3 (Name) and highlighting its name. Then press Return. Press Return again to have the cell range moved.

SEE ALSO

/Worksheet Insert

4

The /File Menu

The /File menu controls all worksheet file functions, including the saving, loading, and combining of worksheets, extracting part of a worksheet in a new file, obtaining directory listings, and importing data from ASCII files.

OPTIONS

- Retrieve
- Save
- Combine
- Xtract
- Erase
- List
- Import
- Directory
- Admin

/FR

The /File Retrieve Command

This command loads the worksheet you specify into the computer's memory, allowing you to make revisions or print it. The worksheet should have been saved in a disk file with the /File Save command.

KEY SEQUENCE

/FR *<filename>* **Return**

Lotus 1-2-3 displays an alphabetical listing of all files saved in the current directory. To select the file desired, move the cursor highlight to it and press Return. You can also type in the file name after invoking this command.

Press F3 to see a full-screen listing of the files in the current directory. If you have saved a worksheet under a file name with an extension other than .WKS or .WK1, you must type in the entire file name, including the extension, in order to retrieve it.

NOTE

When you use /File Retrieve, any worksheet in memory is automatically cleared before another one is loaded. Be sure to save your current worksheet before retrieving another one.

SEE ALSO

/File Directory
/File List

/FS

The /File Save Command

This command saves a Lotus 1-2-3 worksheet in a disk file under a file name of your choice. It saves all data, formulas, display formats, global and range settings, range names, graph definitions (only the latest graph if more than one graph has been defined and each graph has not been named), and the cell pointer position.

KEY SEQUENCE

/FS *<pathname\filename.ext>* **Return**

The first time you use this command to save a worksheet, you must supply a unique file name consisting of no more than eight characters. If you wish to save the file on a disk in a drive other than the default drive or in a directory other than the current directory, type in the complete path name as part of the file name.

Worksheets are automatically given the extension .WK1. You can also enter your own file name extension. If you do, you must enter the complete file name including the period and extension. The program will not automatically display worksheets that do not carry the .WK1 extension as part of their file names.

Using a Password

You can also add a password consisting of up to 15 characters of your choice.

KEY SEQUENCE

/FS *<pathname\filename.ext>* **Spacebar P** *<password>*

You must verify the password by retyping it exactly as you originally entered it, or Lotus 1-2-3 will abort the save operation.

Saving a Previously Saved File

After you have saved a file the first time, Lotus 1-2-3 will supply this file name as the default whenever you save the file again. To accept the file name, press Return.

KEY SEQUENCE

/FS *<filename>* **Return** *<C/R/B>*

To save the file, type **R** for Replace. To abort the save operation, just press Return (**C**, for Cancel is the default). To save the file and copy the old version to *filename.BAK*, press **B** for Backup (Release 2.2 only).

If you wish to save the worksheet under a new file name, simply begin typing the new file name to replace the old one. If the file name has not been used before, you will not be prompted with the Cancel/Replace Backup options. If it has, you will see them. If you use the Replace option, the new worksheet will replace the contents of the one originally stored under that file name.

SEE ALSO

/File Retrieve

/FC

The /File Combine Command

This command copies either an entire worksheet file or a specific range within it into the worksheet currently loaded into memory in the location you specify. It provides the method for combining separate worksheets into one.

KEY SEQUENCE

/FC *<option>* *<E/N>*

Any of the options will work with all of the data in a worksheet (Entire-File) or just a specific range within it (Named/Specified-Range) when performing the copy.

OPTIONS

- Copy
- Add
- Subtract

/File Combine Copy

The Copy option makes a complete copy of all of the data in one worksheet file or in a specified range into another file.

KEY SEQUENCE

After locating the cell pointer at the beginning of the range into which you want the data copied, type

/FCC *<E/N>* *<filename/range>* **Return**

Use the **E** (Entire-File) option to copy all of the data from the specified worksheet into the current file. You can select the *filename* from the displayed listing of files by moving the cursor highlight to it, or you can type in the file name manually. After you press Return, the data is copied into the range beginning at the cell pointer's current position; any existing data in this range is overwritten.

Use the **N** (Named/Specified-Range) option to copy only a particular *range* from the file; you will be prompted to enter the coordinates (cell addresses) of the range to be combined.

/File Combine Add

The Add option copies values contained in one worksheet file and adds them to corresponding cells in another worksheet that also contain values or are empty. This type of /File Combine operation is used when you need to consolidate the values in two or more worksheets. For such a consolidation to operate properly, the spreadsheets must share a common layout and the ranges must be overlaid correctly during the /File Combine Add operation.

/File Combine Add Entire-File

Use this option to combine the values of an entire worksheet in another.

KEY SEQUENCE

After locating the cell pointer at the beginning of the spreadsheet where you want the consolidation to occur, type

/FCAE *<filename>* **Return**

Enter the *filename* of the worksheet whose values you want to include. After Lotus 1-2-3 has finished combining the worksheets, all values whose cells exactly correspond in the two worksheets will be summed in the original worksheet.

NOTES

Any cells that contain values in the second worksheet that correspond to empty cells in the first will now contain the values added from the second (this is because an empty cell carries a value of zero). Any cells that contain values or labels in the original worksheet that correspond to cells that contain labels in the second worksheet will continue to contain their original values or labels (no combining takes place).

When you save the resulting consolidated worksheet, give it a new file name unless you no longer want to maintain a copy of the unconsolidated data in the original worksheet.

/File Combine Add Named/Specified-Range

Use this option to combine the values of a specific range in one worksheet with those in another worksheet file.

KEY SEQUENCE

After locating the cell pointer at the beginning of the range to be summed in the original worksheet file, type

/FCAN *<range>* **Return** *<filename>* **Return**

You must supply the *range* name or coordinates as well as the *filename* in which the range you want to add is stored.

/File Combine Subtract

The Subtract option works much like the Add option in that it copies only values contained in one worksheet file, which in this case are then subtracted from corresponding cells in the other worksheet that also contain values or are empty.

KEY SEQUENCES

When using this command, you have the option of subtracting the values of the entire worksheet file

/FCSE *<filename>* **Return**

or a specified range (by address or range name)

/FCSN *<range>* **Return** *<filename>* **Return**

just as when you use the /File Combine Copy or Add commands.

SEE ALSO

/File Xtract

/FX

The /File Xtract Command

This command copies the range specified in a worksheet into a separate worksheet file by saving it under the file name you supply.

OPTIONS

- Formulas: All formulas used in the specified range are copied to the new file, and their cell references are automatically adjusted to reflect their new location.
- Values: Only the values currently calculated are transferred to the new file. If you wish, you can then copy the range back into the original worksheet by using the /File Combine Copy command.

KEY SEQUENCES

After moving the cell pointer to the beginning of the range to be copied, type

/FX *<F/V>* *<filename>* **Return** *<range>* **Return**

Enter either **F** (to transfer literal values and formulas to the new spreadsheet) or **V** (to transfer values only). You will be prompted to enter a file name for the file you are about to create, and for the range of cells to copy. You can indicate the location of the range by pointing, by entering the appropriate cell addresses, or by entering the range name if you have assigned one to it. After you press Return, Lotus 1-2-3 saves the range, starting at cell A1 in the new worksheet file.

NOTE

When you use the Formulas option with the /FX command, you may find when you retrieve the new worksheet that the cell references in your formulas have become corrupted during the transfer. Cells that are referenced in the original spreadsheet may not have been extracted into the new spreadsheet. In such cases, you may be required to edit key formulas and then copy them throughout the range or add key input cells to correct these errors.

/FE

The /File Erase Command

This command deletes Lotus 1-2-3 files from the current directory. It automatically subdivides files according to type.

OPTIONS

- Worksheet
- Print
- Graph
- Other

/File Erase Worksheet

Use this command to delete a specific worksheet file.

KEY SEQUENCE

/FEW *<filename>* *<Y/N>*

The program displays an alphabetical list of all worksheet files stored in the current directory. You can indicate the name of the file to be deleted either by typing in its name or by moving the highlight to its name and then pressing Return. You can also press F3 to see a full-screen file listing. The program automatically displays worksheet files with both the .WKS and .WK1 extensions. You are then prompted to enter **Y** to carry out the deletion. As No is the default, you can abort this command by pressing Return.

/File Erase Print

Use this command to erase ASCII files given the extension .PRN by Lotus 1-2-3.

KEY SEQUENCE

/FEP *<filename>*

/File Erase Graph

Use this command to erase graph files given the extension .PIC (when saved with the /Graph Save command).

KEY SEQUENCE

/FEG *<filename>*

/File Erase Other

If the file you wish to delete does not carry the .WKS, .WK1, .WK3, .PRN, or .PIC extension, you can still use any of these commands to delete it, but you must type in the complete file name. Use the /File Erase Other command to list and delete any data file, regardless of its extension.

KEY SEQUENCE

/FEO *<filename.ext>*

SEE ALSO

/File List
/File Directory

/FL

The /File List Command

This command obtains a directory listing of Lotus 1-2-3 files from the current directory. It automatically subdivides files according to type.

OPTIONS

- Worksheet
- Print
- Graph
- Other
- Linked (Release 2.2 only)

/File List Worksheet

Use this command to obtain a listing of all your worksheet files.

KEY SEQUENCE

/FLW

The program displays a full-screen alphabetical listing of all worksheet files stored in the current directory. If no worksheet files are found there, the program goes into EDIT mode to allow you to revise the directory.

The directory screen displays both the file name and its extension (.WKS or .WK1). It displays the complete file name, the date and time of creation, and the file size in bytes of the currently highlighted file name. You can move the highlight to obtain these statistics on the various files listed with the cursor movement keys.

/File List Print

Use this command to list all ASCII files given the extension .PRN by Lotus 1-2-3.

KEY SEQUENCE

/FLP

If the ASCII text files do not have the .PRN extension, they will not be included in the directory listing.

/File List Graph

Use this command to list all graph files given the extension .PIC (when saved with the /Graph Save command).

KEY SEQUENCE

/FLG

/File List Other

Use this command to list all data files, regardless of their file name extensions.

KEY SEQUENCE

/FLO

NOTE

After you use any of the /File List command options, press Return to return to the worksheet. You can also press the Esc key to return to the current directory prompt.

/File List Linked (Release 2.2 only)

Use this command to list all files that are linked by formula to the current worksheet. File linking is a new feature in Release 2.2 that allows you to access data in other spreadsheets. See Appendix A for more information about linking.

KEY SEQUENCE

/FLL

SEE ALSO

/File Directory
/File Admin Link-Refresh
/File Admin Table

/FI

The /File Import Command

This command is used to incorporate data saved in an ASCII file into a Lotus 1-2-3 worksheet.

KEY SEQUENCE

After locating the cell pointer at the beginning of the cell range where you want the data copied, type

/FI *<T/N>* *<filename>* **Return**

Be sure that the cell range contains no existing entries that you wish to save. Choose either Text or Numbers by typing **T** or **N**. The program will then prompt you for the name of the file to import. It will also display a line listing of all files in the current directory that have a .PRN file name extension. Select the file name by highlighting it and pressing Return. If your file does not have a .PRN extension, type in its name and press Return (once you begin the file name, the entry line will be cleared).

OPTIONS

- Text
- Numbers

/File Import Text

Use this option when you wish to import both text and numbers that have not been saved in a comma-delimited format in the ASCII file. This option imports each line of ASCII data as a left-aligned label into a single cell starting from the current position of the cell pointer. Each successive line of data is imported into subsequent cells in the same column below the cell pointer. You can use this option with the /Data Parse command to separate individual entries imported as a single label in the worksheet.

/File Import Numbers

Use the Numbers option when

- The ASCII file contains only values.
- The numbers in the file are the only data you want to import.
- The file contains text and numbers saved in the comma-delimited format whereby each entry is separated by a comma, and all text entries are enclosed in a pair of double quotes (single quotes cannot be used).

This option enters each number as a value and each group of text characters enclosed in double quotes as a label. Each comma-delimited entry is placed in its own cell in the same line, starting with the current cell across succeeding columns. Each subsequent line of data is placed in successive rows of the worksheet below the current cell.

SEE ALSO

/Data Parse

/FD

The /File Directory Command

This command allows you to view or change the current directory, which Lotus 1-2-3 uses when saving, retrieving, listing, and erasing files with the associated /File commands. This is the directory that has been set as the default by using the /Worksheet Global Default Directory command.

KEY SEQUENCE

/FD *<pathname>*

To change the directory for the current work session, type in the new directory path name you wish to use. If this directory is located on a new physical drive, be sure to preface the directory path name with the appropriate drive letter.

You can specify any directory that has been set up on a hard disk by giving its full path name. (You can also specify a different hard disk drive, such as D:\, if you have more than one physical device or have set up partitions called C and D within a single hard disk.)

After you set a new current directory, Lotus 1-2-3 will use this directory for saving, retrieving, and listing data files until you change it again by using the same command. When you exit from Lotus 1-2-3 and start the program again, the program will once again use the default directory set with the /Worksheet Global Default Directory command.

SEE ALSO

/Worksheet Global Default Directory

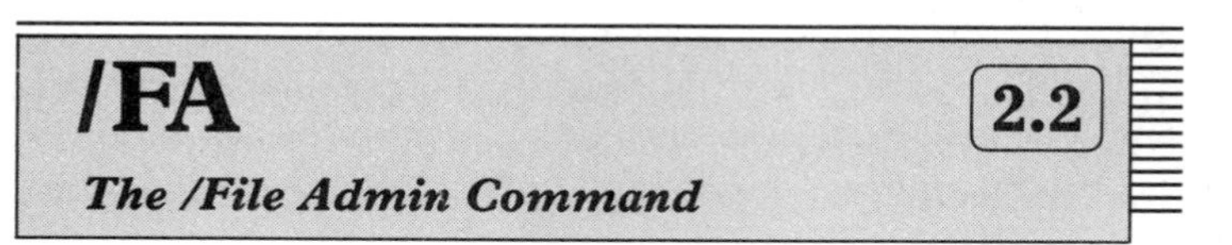

/FA

2.2

The /File Admin Command

This command is used primarily for the new networking features of Release 2.2. It reserves files for your sole use, even though they are available on a disk shared by others. It also updates any linked fields you have in your document. Finally, it allows you to create lists of several different types of files and information about those files in your spreadsheet.

OPTIONS

- Reservation
- Table
- Link-Refresh

/File Admin Reservation

This command is designed for networking environments and lets you control access to a shared file by reserving the ability to save changes to the file. No other user can save the worksheet under the same file name when you have reserved it. A file is reserved automatically the first time it is retrieved, so the reservation must be released in order for another user to save his or her changes.

KEY SEQUENCE

/FAR *<G/R>*

OPTIONS

- Get: Reserves a file so only you can save changes.
- Release: Allows other users to save the file.

/File Admin Table

This command inserts a list of files in your worksheet. You can specify which files are listed by entering a letter at the next menu. This list of files will contain the file name, time and date of modification, and either the file size or the word <DIR>, indicating that that file is a directory.

KEY SEQUENCE

Position the pointer at the upper-left corner of a blank area at least four cells wide and then enter

/FA *<option>*

Once you select an option, the corresponding wildcard string will appear. For example, press **G** (for Graph) and you'll see ⋆.PIC, which specifies all files with the extension .PIC (INCOME.PIC, PROFITS.PIC, etc.). Press Return to accept this string, or change it if you've stored your graphs with a different extension.

Lotus will next ask where you want the upper left-corner of the table. Since you have already positioned the cursor, press Return. The table will be inserted. The first column will be the file name, the second will be the creation date, the third will be the creation time, and the final column will be the size (or <DIR> if the file is a directory).

OPTIONS

- Worksheet: Lists all worksheet files, that is, files that have the .WK1 extension.
- Print: Lists all files with the .PRN extension.
- Graph: Lists all files with the .PIC extension.
- Other: Lists all files in the directory.
- Linked: Lists all files that are linked to the current spreadsheet. (See the discussion on links in the /File Admin Link-Refresh section.)

NOTE

The creation date and time will be formatted as numbers. Use /Range Format Date to format them properly and /Worksheet Column Set-Width if your columns are too narrow to display the formatted values.

File Admin Link-Refresh

KEY SEQUENCE

/FAL

This command is used when you are working on files that are linked to shared files (files that others can use while you are working on your file). A link is an item in your worksheet that refers to an item in another worksheet. For example, you can work on the PROFIT worksheet and use one or more numbers from the COST worksheet. Typically, you exit the PROFIT worksheet to change the COST worksheet. When you do this, the PROFIT worksheet contains the new COST numbers when you work on it again. In a network, however, others can change the COST numbers while you are working with the PROFIT worksheet. You need to tell Lotus when the COST numbers have changed, so that it can update the current (PROFIT) spreadsheet. Use /File Admin Link-Refresh to update these links in the current spreadsheet when you are sharing files.

SEE ALSO

/Range Format Date
/Worksheet Column Set-Width

5

The /Print Menu

The /Print menu controls all aspects of printing Lotus 1-2-3 worksheets. This does not, however, include the printing of graphs created with the program, which is handled by the PrintGraph program and the Allways add-in, new to Release 2.2. This powerful program is covered in depth in Appendix A.

/P

The /Print Command

The /Print command has two basic functions: to print hard copies of data in your worksheets using the text printer you have installed with your system, and to create an ASCII version of the data in your worksheets by creating a new file. The ASCII file created from such a procedure is automatically given the file name extension .PRN.

Most of the time, you will use the /Print menu commands to set up the parameters that define the layout for your printed reports and the data to be included as well as to send the reports to your text printer. Lotus 1-2-3 contains default settings for printing a report on an 8½ × 11-inch page that will be used if you do not change them, so that all you have to do is specify the cell range to be included before using the Align and Go options to begin printing.

KEY SEQUENCE

/P *<P/F>*

OPTIONS

- Printer: uses your text printer to print a report from the worksheet currently in memory.
- File: creates a new text-file version of all or a part of the data in the worksheet. You will be prompted to enter a file name.

Once you have chosen the Printer or File option, you will see the Print settings sheet, with all the current print settings, as illustrated in Figure 5.1. At the top is a menu with the following options:

- Range
- Line
- Page
- Options
- Clear
- Align
- Go
- Quit

The Quit command takes you back to READY mode, which allows you to cycle through its various options without having to keep typing **/PP** or **/PF**.

Range

Use the Range option to designate the cell range to be included in the printout or new disk file.

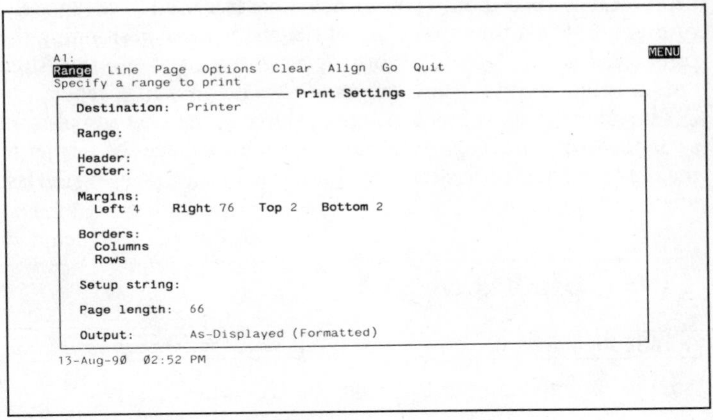

```
A1:                                                              MENU
Range  Line  Page  Options  Clear  Align  Go  Quit
Specify a range to print
                        Print Settings
  Destination:  Printer

  Range:

  Header:
  Footer:

  Margins:
    Left 4    Right 76   Top 2   Bottom 2

  Borders:
    Columns
    Rows

  Setup string:

  Page length:  66

  Output:       As-Displayed (Formatted)
13-Aug-90  02:52 PM
```

Figure 5.1: The Print settings sheet

KEY SEQUENCE

R *<range>* **Return**

You can indicate the *range* by typing in the cell addresses, entering a range name, or pointing out the range.

Depending on the width of the cell range, you may have to modify the right-margin setting with the Options Margins command. The default value for the right margin is 76 characters with a left margin of 4. This means that the maximum line length is 72 characters. If your print range contains more columns than will fit within this line length, you will have to change either the left and right margins or use the appropriate setup string to turn on compressed printing. If you do not, Lotus 1-2-3 will print only those entire columns of information on one page.

The program remembers the print range that you designate and saves it as part of the worksheet file if you use the /File Save command before exiting from the program. To clear the range, use the Clear option.

Line and Page

The Line and Page options are used to advance the paper in the printer either one line at a time or to the next form feed. These commands give you control over the printer from within Lotus 1-2-3 without having to use its controls.

The Line option advances the paper one line and positions the print head at the beginning of the new line. It is used to advance the printer a line at a time to the top of the form. After positioning the print head at the top of the form, you will want to use the Align option before using the Go command to print your next report.

The Page option will advance the printer to the next top-of-form as defined with the Align option. It is used to advance the printer to the top of the next page after the printer has finished printing the last line of a report.

The Options Menu

KEY SEQUENCE

After selecting Printer or File from the /Print menu, type

O *<option>*

OPTIONS

- Header
- Footer
- Margins
- Borders
- Setup
- Pg-Length
- Other
- Quit

Each of these options, with the exception of the Quit command, is discussed in the sections that follow. Typing **Q** to access the Quit command from this menu returns you to the previous level, from which you can use the Align and Go options to begin printing.

The Header Option

This option is used to enter a single-line heading that will be printed on each page of the document. The header line is printed on the first line below the top margin. The default top margin is two lines. Because the body of the report does not begin printing until the fifth line from the top, this leaves a spacing of two lines before the first line of the report. Although you can change the top margin setting by using the Margins Top option, you cannot change the two lines between the header and the first line of the body of the report.

KEY SEQUENCE

After selecting Printer or File from the /Print menu, type

OH *<header text>*

You can use the vertical bar character (¦) to center or right-justify text within the header. One vertical bar placed before the text centers it between the margin settings, and two vertical bars (¦¦) right-justify it with the right-margin setting.

If you wish the current date to appear in the header, type @. If you wish the page number of the report to appear in the header, type #. Otherwise, type the header text exactly as you want it to appear in the report.

The Footer Option

In addition to a report header, you can also define a footer that prints on each page. This text is placed at the bottom of the page, three lines above the end of the page (leaving two blank lines after the last line of the body of the report on the page and two lines after the footer to the last line of the page). Its vertical placement can be changed by using the Margins Bottom option (although the two lines between the last line of the report and the footer cannot be changed).

KEY SEQUENCE

After selecting Printer or File from the /Print menu, type

OF *<footer text>*

You can position text within the footer by using the same technique used to define a header. You can also add the @ symbol to insert the current date or the # symbol to add page numbers.

The Margins Option

The default left and right margins are 4 and 76, respectively. The top and bottom margins are both set to 2 lines (between headers and the top of the page and between footers and the bottom of the page).

KEY SEQUENCE

OM *<option>* *<n>*

For *option*, type the initial letter of the margin you wish to change, or type **N** to clear all margins (this sets the left, top, and bottom margins to 0, and the right to 240). For *n*, type in the new value to be used. As soon as you begin typing, the current value that is displayed will disappear.

Left- and right-margin settings are measured in characters. The value depends on the pitch in effect for printing the report. The standard pitch is pica type (10 characters per inch). Top and bottom margins are measured in lines and depend on the number of lines per inch in effect. (These margins are the space between the header and the top of the page and the footer and the bottom of the page, not the distance between the body of the worksheet and the edge of the paper.) The standard is single spacing (6 lines per inch). Both the pitch and the spacing can be changed by entering the appropriate setup string with the Setup option.

If you are using 14-inch-wide paper to print a report, you will want to use the Margins Right option to set a new right margin of

136 (140 characters in pica type is the maximum that can be accommodated, although you must set Margins Left to 0 to obtain this line length). If you are printing your report in compressed type (see the Setup option) on an 8½ × 11-inch sheet, you would also use this right-margin setting.

OPTIONS

- Left
- Right
- Top
- Bottom
- None (Release 2.2 only)

The Borders Option

This option allows you to specify headings in particular rows or columns of the spreadsheet as borders for the report, meaning that they will be printed on each page of the report.

KEY SEQUENCE

After selecting Printer or File from the /Print menu, type

OB *<C/R>*

OPTIONS

- Columns
- Rows

If you want both a column of labels and some rows of headings to be included on each page, you would use the Borders option twice, once using the Columns option and once using the Rows option.

To specify a row containing column headings that should appear in the top line of the body of the report on every page, use the Rows option. You will be prompted to enter the border rows. To do so, move the cell pointer to one of the cells in the row that contains these headings and press Return. If you want to designate more than one row as border rows, move the cell pointer to the first row, type a period to anchor the cell range, and use the appropriate cursor key to highlight all of the rows you want to include (you do not have to indicate the number of columns as part of this range; this is handled by the right-margin setting).

When you want to specify a column containing row headings to appear on the left of each page of the report, use the Columns option. You indicate the column or columns to be designated as border columns in the same way as you do border rows.

NOTE

When defining border columns, border rows, or both, be sure that you do not include these columns and rows as part of the print range. If you include them as part of the print range, they will be printed twice on the first page of the report.

The Setup Option

This option is used to enter printer control codes for changing such things as the pitch and line spacing, as well as other printing enhancements. Any control codes entered here affect the entire printed report.

KEY SEQUENCE

After selecting Printer or File from the /Print menu, type

OS *<printer control code>*

When you define a setup string, enter its decimal code using three digits preceded by the backslash. For instance, to print a report in compressed print (approximately 17 cpi) on an IBM or Epson dot-matrix printer, you use the decimal code 15. When entering this value as a setup code in Lotus 1-2-3, enter it as **\015**. If you use a printer control code to change to a smaller pitch such as compressed type, you must also remember to increase the right-margin setting, or Lotus 1-2-3 will not print any more columns than it did when using a larger pitch.

You can enter as many printer control codes as you want. When using more than one code, you can enter codes after the initial escape code as ASCII characters rather than entering their decimal equivalents preceded by the backslash and a zero, making sure that there are no spaces between them. For instance, you could enter the codes to set the pitch to 8 lines per inch on an Epson printer (Esc 0) as **\0270** or as **\027\048**.

The Pg-Length Option

This option is used most frequently when you are printing reports on paper longer than 11 inches. It can also be used to fit more lines per page on an $8^1/_2 \times 11$-inch page.

KEY SEQUENCE

After selecting Printer or File from the /Print menu, type

OP *<n>*

The default setting is 66 lines per page (with a top and bottom margin of 5 lines each, this leaves 56 lines per page when using single spacing). You can change this to any value between 1 and 100.

If you have changed the lines-per-inch setting with a setup code, you can adjust this value to accommodate the number of lines according to whether you have set the spacing up or down. If you are trying to fit a few more lines on a one-page report using single spacing, you should consider using the Other Unformatted option to remove page breaks and headers and footers to accommodate the extra lines.

The Other Option

This option is attached to a menu of choices that allow you to modify the formatting or contents of the printed report.

KEY SEQUENCE

After selecting Printer or File from the /Print menu, type

OO *<option>*

OPTIONS

- **As-Displayed**
- Cell-Formulas
- **Formatted**
- Unformatted

The As-Displayed and Formatted Options

The first and third options on this menu, As-Displayed and Formatted, are the defaults used by the program whenever you print a worksheet to a disk file or the printer. With As-Displayed in effect, the contents of the cells in the print range specified are printed just as they appear on the screen, except that the column and row borders are not included. With Formatted in effect, the program pages the report as specified by the Pg-Length and lines per page settings and includes all headers and footers that you have defined. The As-Displayed option is used to restore this program default whenever you have previously used the Cell-Formulas option. The Formatted option is used to restore this program default whenever you have previously used the Unformatted option.

The Cell-Formulas Option

The Cell-Formulas option causes the contents of the cells in the print range to be printed as a line listing, rather than as a formatted report as displayed on the screen. The literal contents (including any formulas used) of each cell in the range are printed on a separate line of the report. This command is most often used to document the complete contents of the worksheet. In it, each cell entry is printed on an individual line across each row, down the entire worksheet.

The Unformatted Option

The Unformatted option prints a copy of the report without using the Pg-Length value to break pages or the top and margin settings, including any header or footer that has been defined. This option is used most often to remove these formatting commands before printing the worksheet to an ASCII file (using /Print File as the initial command) that will be used in another application program, such as a word processor.

It is also useful when printing a report that contains only a few more lines than will fit within the standard page length. Using the Unformatted option suppresses the page break at the Pg-Length setting, allowing those few extra lines of the report to fit on a single page because no space is retained for either the header or footer.

Clear

Because the program remembers all the print settings that you set up from the /Print menu, you may find it convenient to use the Clear option when setting up a report that uses a different print range, different format, or both.

KEY SEQUENCE

After selecting Printer or File from the /Print menu, type

OC *<option>*

OPTIONS

- All
- Range
- Borders
- Format

The Clear All Option

Using this option clears all print settings back to their program default values. This includes the print range, margin settings, borders defined, and formatting specified.

The Clear Range Option

This option resets the print range that has been defined in the worksheet. If all you need to do is designate a new part of the spreadsheet to be printed, using the Clear Range option makes this easier to accomplish. It leaves all of the other formatting options in effect while freeing the cell pointer, so that you can move to the new area before using the /Range command to indicate the new cell range to be used.

The Clear Borders Option

This option clears any previously set borders. It allows you to print a copy of the report using the same print range and other formatting settings, but without repeating any columns or rows on subsequent pages.

The Clear Format Option

This option returns the format settings, including the page length and the margins, to their default values. It also clears any printer control codes that were entered by using the Options Setup option.

Align and Go

The Align and Go options are used together when sending a report to the printer. The Align option tells the program that the print head is currently at the top of the form. It then uses this position to page the report according to the number of lines per page (set with the Pg-Length option). The Go option actually begins the printing process. If you need to suspend printing for any reason after that, press Ctrl-Num Lock. If you wish to abort the printing process, press Ctrl-Scroll Lock.

If you are using the /Print File option to create an ASCII file, you do not need to use the Align option before the Go option. ASCII files are not paged, regardless of the Pg-Length setting in effect.

NOTES

You can also enter setup codes directly into the print range that produce special print enhancements affecting only a particular number of lines in the report, rather than the entire report, as is the case when you use the the Options Setup command on the /Print menu.

To enter a particular setup string directly into the worksheet, position the cell pointer in the leftmost column of the print range, in the row where the print enhancement is to begin. Then insert a new row (with the /Worksheet Insert Row command) and enter two vertical bars (¦¦) followed by the setup string to be used.

SEE ALSO

/Worksheet Page

6

The /Graph Menu

The /Graph menu controls all aspects of creating graphs from existing spreadsheets. You also use it to view graphed results on the screen, name individual graphs that are to be saved as part of the worksheet file, and save graphs in separate graph files. You cannot, however, print graphs from this menu. All graph printing is controlled from the separate PrintGraph or Allways programs. See Appendix A for information about Allways.

/G

The /Graph Command

KEY SEQUENCE

/G *<option>*

When you press **/G**, the Graph settings sheet (illustrated in Figure 6.1) appears. It shows all of the current graph settings, along with a menu of options.

To create a Lotus 1-2-3 graph, you need to specify only two elements from the /Graph menu: the type of graph by using the Type option (Line graph is the default supplied if you do not use this option) and the cell range or ranges containing the values to be graphed. You define each cell range as a specific data variable by designating it as an alphabetical letter between A and F. You designate the labels or values that identify the X axis by using the X option to define the appropriate cell range in the worksheet. In Release 2.2, the new /Graph Group command will define all of your ranges for

```
A1:                                                                    MENU
Type  X  A  B  C  D  E  F  Reset  View  Save  Options  Name  Group  Quit
Line  Bar  XY  Stack-Bar  Pie
                              Graph Settings
 Type: Line                   Titles: First
                                      Second
 X:                                   X axis
 A:                                   Y axis
 B:
 C:                                               Y scale:     X scale:
 D:                                   Scaling     Automatic    Automatic
 E:                                   Lower
 F:                                   Upper
                                      Format      (G)          (G)
 Grid: None         Color: No         Indicator   Yes          Yes

    Legend:                 Format:   Data labels:             Skip: 1
 A                          Both
 B                          Both
 C                          Both
 D                          Both
 E                          Both
 F                          Both
13-Aug-90  02:53 PM
```

Figure 6.1: The Graph settings sheet

OPTIONS

- Type
- X A B C D E F
- Reset
- View
- Save
- Options
- Name
- Group (Release 2.2. only)
- Quit

you if they are grouped together. All you have to do is keep your data in adjacent rows or columns.

After defining the basic graph, you can add many types of enhancements by using the commands available from the /Graph Options menu. From there, you can add titles, legends, or grid lines to your graph, change the scaling of its X or Y axis, format its values, set the graph to display in color (if you have a color monitor), and specify labels to identify the data points for each data variable.

When creating a graph, you can use the View option to view its current state if your computer is equipped with a graphics card. Lotus 1-2-3 switches the full-screen view from the spreadsheet to the graph. To return to the /Graph menu and the spreadsheet from the graph display, you can press any key. If you use the Quit option on the /Graph menu to return to READY mode to make some changes to the worksheet, you can view the graph currently defined by pressing the Graph key (F10).

The use of all the /Graph menu options, with the exception of the Quit commands attached to various submenus, is discussed in the individual sections that follow. The Quit commands on these menus all work just like pressing the Esc key: they back you up to the previous menu level.

/Graph Type

This command is used to assign one of the five graph types to the graph you are building.

KEY SEQUENCE

/GT *<option>*

To choose a new graph type, type the first letter of the graph name.

- **Line**
- Bar
- XY
- Stack-Bar
- Pie

You can use the Type command to change the graph type at any time after defining it. This allows you to view the information graphed in another format.

Line Graph

A line graph represents your data as individual data points connected by lines. Each data point represents the magnitude of the value in that data variable compared against the Y scale of the graph. Each data variable used in the graph is defined by assigning a range of values in the spreadsheet to a particular data variable letter from A to F.

The values in each data variable are given different symbols to differentiate them in the graph. These are assigned according to the letter of the data variable used.

To change the way a line graph is displayed to show just the symbols or lines, use the Format option attached to the /Graph Options menu. Use the Legend option on the /Graph Options menu to create a legend that labels each of the symbols used.

Bar Graph

A bar graph represents data as individual vertical bars, each one showing the magnitude of the value compared to the Y scale of the graph. Each data variable used in the graph is defined by assigning a range of values in the spreadsheet to a particular data variable letter from A to F.

The bars representing individual data values in each data variable are given different cross-hatching fill patterns or colors to differentiate them from one another in the graph. These are assigned according to the letter of the data variable used. If you have a color monitor, you can have the bars of the graph displayed in different colors by using the Color option on the /Graph Options menu. Use the Legend option on the /Graph Options menu to create a legend that labels each of the fill types or colors used.

XY Graph

An XY graph uses numerical values for both the X and Y axes of the graph. Each data point in the graph is plotted according to pairs of values, one set for the X axis and another for the Y axis.

Typically, an XY graph illustrates only one data variable, with the symbols representing the data points shown without any connecting lines between them. The magnitude of the data points on the Y scale is plotted by using the values in a cell range defined as the first variable with the A command on the /Graph menu. The magnitude of the data points on the X axis is plotted by using the values in a cell range defined as the X-axis range with the X command on the /Graph menu. Use the /Data Sort command to arrange the A data variable values in ascending order before creating the graph.

To display an XY graph showing only the symbols, use the Format option attached to the /Graph Options menu. Because only one data variable is represented by each pair of values in the spreadsheet, only the first type of symbol is used and a legend is not required.

StackBar Graph

A stacked-bar graph is a special type of vertical bar graph in which the value for each data variable is accumulated to determine the magnitude of the bar on the Y axis. There are as many stacks in a single vertical bar as there are data variables defined. Each stack is given its own fill pattern or color to differentiate it within each bar. The relative size of the stack represents the percentage of each value to the total of all values.

The position of the stack in each bar and the type of fill pattern or color used is determined by the order in which the data variables are defined using the letter commands A to F on the /Graph menu. Use the Legend option on the /Graph Options menu to create a legend that labels each of the fill types or colors used.

Pie Graph

The Pie option on the /Graph Type menu is used to represent data as a pie chart. This type of graph uses only one data variable, assigned with the A command on the /Graph menu, for a single range of values in the spreadsheet. Each value in the data variable is computed as a percentage of the total of all values used. This percentage is represented by an individual segment of a circle representing the total, or 100 percent.

Lotus 1-2-3 automatically displays the percentage it calculates for each segment. To add labels, use the X-axis range (the X command on the /Graph menu) to assign the labels from a cell range in the spreadsheet. Negative values in the range are graphed as though they were entered as positive values, displaying their segments incorrectly as positive percentages.

Fill Patterns and Exploded Pie Graphs

You can assign different fill patterns to each segment of the pie as well as explode specific segments to emphasize them in the graph. To do this, you must enter numbers between 1 and 6 (used as code numbers for the various shading patterns available) in the worksheet and assign the range containing these values as the B data variable for the pie chart. To explode a segment, add 100 to the shading value used.

The /Graph X A B C D E F Commands

The group of commands represented by alphabetical letters is used to assign the values in your spreadsheet that are to be included in the graph you are creating.

The X-Axis Range

The X command is used to designate the X-axis range. The use for this command varies according to the type of graph you are creating:

- In line, bar, and stacked-bar graphs, the X-axis range designates a cell range containing labels that are to be displayed along the

X axis of the graph. Each label is associated with a specific tick mark and identifies the data in each data variable graphed.

- In an XY graph, the X-axis range designates a cell range that contains one set of the pairs of values that determine the placement of the data points along the X axis.
- In a pie chart, the X-axis range designates a cell range containing the labels used to identify each section of the pie. If you specify an X-axis range, these labels are placed immediately before the percentages displayed by the program, next to the appropriate segment.

If you are using this option to define a range of values for an XY graph, the values contained in the range are placed below each tick mark and can be formatted with the /Graph Options Scale Format option.

Data Variables A–F

The commands A, B, C, D, E, and F are used to designate the cell ranges in the worksheet that contain the various values to be graphed. You can specify up to six different ranges, each representing a letter variable from A to F. You define each cell range containing values to be graphed by first typing the letter of the data variable and then indicating the range of cells that contains the values to be used. You specify only as many data variables as you have sets of values to be graphed in the worksheet. The letter of the data variable determines its order in the graph, with A being the first data variable and F being the sixth.

When Lotus 1-2-3 creates the graph, it plots the value in each data variable against the scale of the Y axis, using the symbols appropriate to the type of graph selected. The exception to this is the pie chart, which has no X or Y axis and requires only an A data variable to be assigned (except when assigning fill types to various segments of the pie chart).

/Graph Reset

KEY SEQUENCE

/GR *<option>*

OPTIONS

- Graph
- X A B C D E F
- Ranges (Release 2.2 only)
- Options (Release 2.2 only)
- Quit

The /Graph Reset Graph Option

This option clears all previously defined graph options, returning all values to their default settings. You need to use this option only when the graph you are creating is so different from the previous one that very few or none of the previous settings apply to it.

The /Graph Reset X and A–F Options

Use the individual letter options, X and A to F, to clear the cell range containing the values assigned to a specific data variable. Doing this allows you to assign new values while retaining some of the common settings, such as legends and titles.

The /Graph Reset Ranges Option (Release 2.2 only)

This option clears all of the data ranges you have defined. Use this option to clear all of your variables when you want to start over and graph a different set of data, using the same format as your previous graph.

The /Graph Reset Options Option (Release 2.2 only)

This choice clears all of the options you specified for your graph. It clears legends, titles, data labels, and all other Options settings. You will probably use this option when you want to make a graph more simple.

/Graph View

This command allows you to see the graph on the screen at various stages during its creation.

KEY SEQUENCE

/GV

Whenever you type **V** from the /Graph menu, the menu and spreadsheet display is replaced by a new screen showing only the current graph. To return to the /Graph menu, press any key.

If you have used the Quit command from the /Graph menu to return to the spreadsheet, press the Graph key (F10) to display the graph.

/Graph Save

This command is used to save the current graph in a separate file under the file name you assign to it. This file name is automatically appended with the file name extension .PIC. This marks it as a special file that can be printed using the PrintGraph program. If you do not use the /Graph Save command on a graph, you will not be able to print it. The graph will, however, be saved as part of the worksheet file if you use the /File Save command before exiting from the program.

KEY SEQUENCE

/GS *<filename>* **Return**

The program will display a line listing of all the graph file names currently in use. To give your graph a new name, type it in. You must obey the same file-naming conventions as when saving a regular worksheet file. The graph will be saved in whatever directory is currently set as the default.

The /Graph Options Menu

The Options command provides the most complex menu hierarchy on the /Graph menu. The commands that you access through it control all aspects of graph definition beyond selecting the graph type and the data to be graphed, naming graphs, and saving graphs.

KEY SEQUENCE

/GO *<options>*

OPTIONS

- Legend
- Format
- Titles
- Grid
- Scale
- Color
- B&W
- Data-Labels
- Quit

The Quit command allows you to choose among the various options you wish to assign to the graph you are creating without having to preface each command with O for Options. To view your graph at any stage in its development, type **QV**.

The /Graph Options Legend Option

This option assigns labels that identify each of the graph elements used to represent the data variables in your graph.

KEY SEQUENCE

/GOL *<variable/R>* *<label>*

The command is attached to a menu listing of the possible data *variables* from A to F and a Range option. To assign a legend for each of your data variables, you can type its letter and then give the description you wish to assign to it. In Release 2.2, you can also use the /Graph Options Legend Range command to assign a range of labels or legends to the variables. This is often faster than specifying each variable and legend separately. Simply enter all of your legends into a cell range, select this option, and specify the range of legends. The first legend in the range will be assigned to variable A, the second to variable B, and so on. When entering a legend, you can type in the descriptive *label* (up to 19 characters long) or reference a cell in the spreadsheet that contains the appropriate label. To use a label existing in a cell, preface the cell address with a backslash followed by the cell address (as in **\D10**). After you assign a legend to a particular data variable by letter, you are returned immediately to the /Graph Options menu. To assign the next legend, you must retype **L** before you type its letter.

The /Graph Options Format Option

This option allows you to change the way Lotus 1-2-3 represents the data in line and XY graphs.

KEY SEQUENCE

/GOF *<variable>* *<format>*

OPTIONS

- Graph
- Quit
- X A B C D E F

To change all of the data variables, select the Graph option. To change only a specific data variable in a line or XY graph, select the appropriate letter for the data variable. Using the Quit option returns you immediately to the /Graph Options menu.

After you choose which data variable to change, you are presented with another set of menu options:

- Lines
- Both
- Symbols
- Neither

If you do not want lines connecting each data point in a data variable, you can change the format of the data variable by selecting the Symbols option. To suppress the use of the symbols and show only the line for each data variable, select the Lines option.

To return a data variable to its default of displaying both symbols and the connecting lines, use the Both option. The last option, Neither, suppresses the display of the data points in the graph.

The /Graph Options Titles Option

This option allows you to add four different types of titles to your graph: two general titles (First and Second), a title for the X axis, and one for the Y axis.

KEY SEQUENCE

/GOT *<option>* *<title>*

OPTIONS

- First
- X-Axis
- Second
- Y-Axis

The First Option

Use the First option to enter a general title for the graph that appears on the first line. When prompted for the title, you can type it in or reference a cell in the spreadsheet that already contains the appropriate text by typing \ and the cell address (such as **A2**). The first title of the graph is printed in a larger font than is used to print the rest of the text in the graph (although this is not evident when viewing a graph on the screen).

The Second Option

Add a second graph title by using the Second option. This title is automatically placed below the first title with a blank line left between them. Both the first and second titles are centered over the entire graph and can contain a maximum of 36 characters. This title can be entered in the same manner as the first title.

The X-Axis Option

The X-Axis option lets you add a title summarizing the content of the labels or values assigned as the X-axis range. This title is centered on its own line below the tick mark labels and above the line containing the graph legend, if any has been defined. It is entered in the same way that you enter the first and second titles.

The Y-Axis Option

The last type of title is a Y-axis title. This title summarizes the content of the values on the Y axis of the graph. It is rotated 90 degrees so that it reads up the left side of the graph. This title is centered between the X-axis reference line and the top border line of the graph. You can enter this title by typing in the text or by referencing a cell that already contains a suitable label, just as you enter the other types of titles.

The /Graph Options Grid Option

This option is used to add grid lines that form a background on the screen similar to that of graph paper.

KEY SEQUENCE

/GOG *<option>*

OPTIONS

- Horizontal: adds grid lines that run horizontally across the graph, extending from each tick mark on the Y axis to the opposite border line.
- Vertical: adds grid lines that run vertically up from each tick mark on the X axis to the top border line of the graph.
- Both: adds both types of grid lines to the graph.
- Clear: removes any grid lines that you previously defined for the graph with the other options.

The /Graph Options Scale Option

This option has several uses.

- You can use its Manual, Upper, and Lower options to set new upper and lower values for either the X or Y scale of the graph.
- You can use its Format option to format the values on the X or Y axis, using the same types of formats you've used to change the display of the values in the spreadsheet (with either the /Worksheet Global Format or the /Range Format command).
- You can use the Indicator option to suppress the display of the (*Thousands*) label indicator or any other scale notation Lotus 1-2-3 uses when values along an axis are best represented in other units, such as (*Millions*) or, above a million, (*Times 10E9*).
- You can use its Skip option to have the program display some of the labels or values in the X-axis range at an interval that you set by number, such as displaying the label for every third tick mark on the X axis.

KEY SEQUENCE

/GOS *<option>*

OPTIONS

- Y Scale
- X Scale
- Skip

Choose the Y Scale or X Scale option when you want to change the upper or lower value displayed for either axis or when you want to format the values of one of these axes. To use the Indicator option, you must choose the Y Scale option first, as the Indicator option affects only the Y axis.

The Skip Command

To restrict the display of the labels or values in the cell range defined as the X-axis range, choose the Skip command. You will then be prompted to enter a value between 1 and 8192 to be used as the skip factor. For instance, if you enter **5**, the program will display only every fifth label or value in the cell range below the appropriate tick mark on the X axis. All of the other tick marks will still be displayed at the bottom of the graph, although they will no longer be labeled. This command is used to avoid the overlapping of X-axis labels that sometimes occurs when you are graphing many values.

Specifying the X Scale or Y Scale

After you choose either the Y Scale or X Scale option, the following menu of options is displayed:

OPTIONS

- Automatic
- Manual
- Lower
- Upper
- Format
- Indicator
- Quit

To set new values for the axis, choose either the Lower or Upper option, whichever applies. In either case, you will be prompted to enter the new value. After doing so and pressing Return, you will be returned to this menu.

When you change the scale values, you must choose the Manual option before leaving this menu to have the program use your new scaling values. If you do not, you will find that the scale has not been changed when you next view the graph. You can also choose the Manual option before using the Lower or Upper option. To return the scale to the values automatically set up when Lotus 1-2-3 generated the graph, select the Automatic option.

To add one of the formats used by the program to the values on one of the graph scales, use the Format option. You are presented with a menu of format options identical in form and use to that found on the /Range Format menu. When using formats such as Currency and Fixed, you must enter the number of decimal places to be displayed. However, after you choose the format and indicate the number of decimal places (if applicable), you need not specify the cell range to which it applies. It is automatically applied to the scale you specified before accessing the Format option.

Choose the Indicator option to remove the (*Thousands*) or some other indicator label that Lotus 1-2-3 automatically adds when it scales the Y axis and graphs values that contain thousands or larger values. When you use this command, you are presented with Yes and No options. Choose No to suppress the display of the indicator label. You can later restore it to the graph by accessing the Indicator option again, this time choosing the Yes option.

The /Graph Options Color and B&W Options

The Color option changes the display of graphs from black and white (the program's default) to color. If you have a color monitor and a color/graphics card, you will want to use this option to enhance the on-screen display of your graphs. However, if you do not have a color printer, you will want to use the B&W option to change the setting back to black and white before saving your bar and stacked-bar graphs with the /Graph Save command. Otherwise, the bars will be printed solid black instead of with different cross-hatching patterns.

If you have a monochrome monitor and a color printer, you will want to do just the opposite. Keep the default set to B&W until you are ready to save the graphs in their own files. Then select the Color option before using the /Graph Save command. You can then use the B&W option to restore the black-and-white setting for viewing your graphs on the screen.

KEY SEQUENCES

/GOC
/GOB

The /Graph Options Data-Labels Option

This option allows you to select a range of cells in the spreadsheet that contains labels you wish to be displayed in the graph next to their graphic representation.

KEY SEQUENCE

/GOD *<data variable/G>* *<range>* *<C/R>* *<option>*

OPTIONS

- A B C D E F
- Quit
- Group (Release 2.2 only)

From this menu, you can type the letter of the *data variable* to which your data labels are to be applied. After you select the data variable by letter, you are prompted to indicate the cell *range* in the spreadsheet that contains the labels. You can define this range by typing its cell addresses, using a range name, or pointing.

In Release 2.2, you can specify all of the data labels for your graph at once by selecting the Group option on this menu. Next, specify the range that contains the data labels. Finally, enter either **C** or **R** to tell Lotus that the data labels are arranged by columns or by rows. It will assign the rows or columns of data labels to the variables in order, top-to-bottom for rows or right-to-left for columns.

After defining the range, you will receive a new menu of *options* used to tell the program where to position the data labels in relation to the data points (data labels used in bar and stacked-bar graphs are automatically placed above the bar when the value is positive and below the bar when the value is negative):

- Center
- Right
- Left
- Below
- Above

To have the data labels positioned above the data points, choose the Above option. If you do not specify any other placement, Lotus 1-2-3 will center the label above each data point. The same is true if you use the Below option to have the labels displayed underneath the data points (this would be done only if you have used the /Graph Options Format Symbols command for the data variable). The Left and Right options place the data label immediately to either side of the data point.

Once you have finished defining data labels for all the data variables that you wish and have specified their relative positions, use the Quit command to return to the /Graph Options menu (to view the graph directly, type **QQV**).

/Graph Name

This command is used to name different graphs created in a single worksheet, to make a new graph current, or to delete graphs that have already been defined and named from the worksheet.

KEY SEQUENCE

/GN *<option>* *<name>*

OPTIONS

- Use
- Create
- Delete
- Reset
- Table

The /Graph Name Use Option

This option is used to make a new graph current. When you access it, you are prompted for the name of the graph to make current. The program shows a list of graph names in use. To select the one you wish to make current, use the arrow keys to highlight it and then press Return. After you make a graph current, you can make changes to it by using the other /Graph menu options. That graph will be the one that is displayed whenever you use the /Graph View command or press the Graph key (F10) from within the spreadsheet.

The /Graph Name Create Option

This option is used to assign a name to the graph that you have created. The name you assign can have up to 15 characters and can contain spaces just like a range name. In fact, graph names are saved as part of the worksheet file, just as range names are saved when you use the /File Save command (if you assign names with the Create option but do not save the file with /FS, your graph settings will not be saved).

When you assign graph names, be careful not to reuse a name already given to another graph. Lotus 1-2-3 will not prompt you before overwriting the settings for the original graph with those you have just defined, as it does when you inadvertently save a worksheet file under a file name that is in use.

You do not have to name a graph to save its settings in a worksheet if it is the only graph you have created. It is automatically considered to be the current graph, and its settings will be saved even without a name as long as you use the /File Save command before exiting from the program. However, you must name a graph to save its definition if you are going to define other graphs from the same worksheet.

The /Graph Delete Option

This option is used to remove a graph definition from a worksheet file. When you access the Delete command, you are prompted for the name of the graph to delete. The program shows you a listing of the graph names in use. To delete a particular graph, use the arrow keys to highlight it and then press Return. Lotus 1-2-3 will not prompt you for confirmation but will go ahead and erase the settings for the graph as soon as you press Return. However, if the named graph was previously saved on disk with the /File Save command, the graph will still exist there until you use /File Save again.

The /Graph Name Reset Option

This option erases the graph definitions for all named graphs. When you use Reset, all graph names are removed without any confirmation. Use this option with care, because as soon as you type **R** for Reset, all graphs are immediately deleted.

The /Graph Name Table Option

In Release 2.2, you can create a table of graphs that you have named by selecting the /Graph Name Table option. It will insert a two-column list of graph names, and types at the location you specify.

/Graph Group

With Release 2.2, you can now create graphs much more quickly than before with the new /Graph Group command. It will define all of your data ranges for you, with just a little input.

KEY SEQUENCE

/GG *<range>* *<C/R>*

To use this command, all of your data ranges, including the X range, must be in adjacent columns or rows. Furthermore, they must be in order; the X range must be to the left of or above the A range, and so on. After you select /GG, specify this data range. Lotus will ask if this range is arranged in columns (Columnwise) or rows (Rowwise) and then define all of your data ranges that were specified.

7

The /Data Menu

The functions of the commands on the /Data menu are among the most varied of any Lotus 1-2-3 menu.

OPTIONS

- Fill: automatic generation of sequences of numbers.
- Table: multiple formula calculation for extended what-if analysis.
- Sort: sorting text and data in cell ranges.
- Query: database management.
- Distribution: statistical analysis.
- Matrix: statistical analysis.
- Regression: statistical analysis.
- Parse: splitting long label entries in single cells into separate cells containing individual data items.

/DF

The /Data Fill Command

This command automatically enters a sequence of numbers in either ascending or descending order in a specified range of cells.

KEY SEQUENCE

After positioning the cell pointer in the cell where you want the number sequence to begin, type

/DF *<range>* **Return** *<start>* **Return**
<step> **Return** *<stop>* **Return**

The cell *range* where the values are to be entered can be specified by typing the cell addresses or range name or pointing to the cells. Though this range most often consists of cells in a single column or row of the worksheet, the /Data Fill command will work with two-dimensional cell ranges. When entering values in such a range, Lotus 1-2-3 always numbers down each column instead of across each row.

Start, step, and stop values need not be integers or constants—you can enter formulas, mathematical expressions, and functions that return numbers.

The *start* value is the number entered in the first cell of the specified range. The program supplies the default value of 0. To specify a new value, type it in.

The *step* value determines by how much each value in the sequence is increased or decreased (default: increase by 1). To create a series of numbers that decrease, specify the step value as a negative number.

The *stop* value determines the highest value entered in the sequence. The default is 8191. Most of the time you can accept this default value when specifying ascending number progressions by pressing Return: the cell range used will control the highest (or lowest) number generated in the sequence. Specify a lower value if you want the /Data Fill command to stop after reaching a particular value that might occur before the cell range is entirely filled. When generating a decreasing number list, you must enter a stop number that is as low as or lower than the last value that will be generated in the specified range.

SEE ALSO

/Data Table
/Data Distribution

/DT

The /Data Table Command

This command allows you to perform extended what-if analysis in a spreadsheet whose results are saved in tabular form. Lotus 1-2-3 creates the data table by substituting each of the various input variables listed in the table into a master formula. Because the results calculated by testing the new input variables in the formula are stored as values, the table is not subject to further recalculation in the normal way. Lotus 1-2-3 allows you to generate a new data table in the same area of the worksheet by entering new input values and then pressing the Table key (F8).

KEY SEQUENCE

/DT *<option>*

OPTIONS

- 1: creates a one-input data table.
- 2: creates a two-input data table.
- Reset: clears all previously defined data-table settings for either type 1 or type 2 tables. The Reset option is quite useful when you are generating subsequent tables from the same spreadsheet or database and you are using the pointing method to indicate the table range, input variables, or both.

/Data Table 1

To generate a one-input data table with the /Data Table 1 command, you must establish a list of the input variables to be tested in the master formula in a single column of the worksheet. These values must be in a contiguous cell range, although they need not be arranged in any particular order. You can often use the /Data Fill command to have the program generate these input variables for you rather than entering the values manually.

The formula in which these values are to be tried must be entered in the column immediately to the right of the input variables and one row above the cell containing the first input variable.

KEY SEQUENCE

After you enter the input variables and the master formula, type

/DT1 *<range>* **Return** *<input cell>* **Return**

The table *range* must include all of the rows and columns that contain input variables and the master formula or formulas. This means that the first cell of the table range is an empty cell to the left of the cells containing your formulas and just above the list of the input variables. The last cell in this range is defined by the junction of the column of the last master formula and the row of the last input variable. When indicating this range, you can type in the cell addresses or use pointing.

After you indicate the table range and press Return, you will be asked to designate the cell address of the *input cell.* This cell can be any cell located outside the table range you have just defined. You may find it convenient to indicate the address of the cell in the spreadsheet that contains the input value used in the original formula. It does not matter whether this cell contains a value; the program will restore the original value after generating the data table.

After you indicate the cell address of the input cell (by typing in its address or pointing to it), press Return once more to have the program calculate the results and enter them in the table.

Using /Data Table 1 with Databases

When you generate a one-input data table using a database, you follow much the same procedure as when using it to create a what-if table in a spreadsheet. There are, however, some differences:

- The master formula or formulas contain database statistical functions.
- The list of input variables represents valid field entries that determine the criterion by which the database statistical functions are calculated.
- The input cell will be the cell beneath the field name in the criterion range that matches the field from which the input variables are chosen.

When you use the /Data Table 1 command to produce summary statistics from a database, the program substitutes each input variable into the input cell in the criterion range and calculates the results returned by the particular database statistical function based on matches to this value in the appropriate field of the database.

/Data Table 2

When you use the /Data Table 2 command, you must use a slightly different table layout from that used for /Data Table 1. Because only one master formula can be used in this type of data table, it is always located in the first cell of the table range, the one usually left blank when using the /Data Table 1 command. It can be entered in the same way as master formulas are in the first type of table, either by direct reference or literal input.

This type of table requires that you list two different sets of input variables to be tested in the formula. The first set of values are entered in the same column as the master formula, starting with the row directly below it. The second set of input variables are entered in the same row as the master formula, starting with the column immediately to its right. The table range includes all the cells included within the columns and rows used to enter these two sets of input variables.

KEY SEQUENCE

After you enter the master formula and the two sets of input variables, type

/DT2 *<input>* **Return** *<input cell 1>* **Return**
<input cell 2> **Return**

First indicate the table *range.* After you define this range and press Return, you will then be asked to designate *input cell 1*. It must be a cell that is not part of the table range, where the program can temporarily store the first input variables listed below the master formula. After you indicate this cell address and press Return, you will be prompted to indicate *input cell 2.* This must also be a cell outside the table range and different from input cell 1. This is where the second set of input variables located to the right of the master formula can be temporarily stored.

The input cells can be empty or can contain data. If they contain values, 1-2-3 will restore the values after generating the data table.

After you define input cell 2 and press Return, the program will calculate the formula using all of the input variables listed in the table. The results of these calculations will be entered into the data table in their appropriate column and row positions.

Using /Data Table 2 with Databases

When you generate a two-input data table using a database, you follow much the same procedure as when using it to create a what-if table in a spreadsheet. There are, however, some differences:

- The master formula contains database statistical functions.
- The two sets of input variables represent valid field entries from two different fields in the database that determine the criterion by which the database statistical function is calculated.
- The first input cell will be the cell beneath the field name in the criterion range that matches the field from which the first set of input variables is chosen. The second input cell will be the cell beneath the field name in the criterion range that matches the field from which the second set of input variables is chosen.

When you use the /Data Table 2 command to produce cross-tabulated statistics from a database, the program substitutes each input pair of variables into the input cells in the criterion range and calculates the results returned by the particular database statistical function based on matches to these values in their appropriate fields in the database.

/DS

The /Data Sort Command

This command allows you to sort data in the worksheet in either ascending or descending order according to a specific field or column in the range of values.

The column (or field) that controls the order in which the records are arranged is referred to as a *key*. The Lotus 1-2-3 /Data Sort command allows you to specify up to two keys that determine the final sorted order.

When sorting data in a spreadsheet or database, you must be careful when the range to be used contains cells referenced by formulas outside that range. All cell references are adjusted within the data range that is sorted, while cell references in dependent formulas outside the specified range are not affected. As a result, formulas outside the sorted data range may no longer refer to the correct value because it has been moved to a new cell position.

You can change the sorting order used by the /Data Sort command. It now supports three different collating sequences:

1. Numbers last.
2. Numbers first, which is the program default.

3. ASCII, which places numbers before uppercase letters, with lowercase letters following all uppercase letters.

To change to a different collating order, you must use the Advanced Options on the Lotus Access System Install Menu.

KEY SEQUENCE

/DS *<option>*

When you press **/DS**, the Sort settings sheet (illustrated in Figure 7.1) appears, showing the cell addresses of the data range and sort keys (primary and secondary), the sort order for each key, and a menu.

OPTIONS

- Data-Range
- Primary-Key
- Secondary-Key
- Reset
- Go
- Quit

To perform your first sorting operation, you must use at least the Data-Range and Primary-Key options before using the Go option to have the program perform the sort.

Data Range

The Data-Range option defines the location of the data to be sorted. The range should include only the actual values and/or labels to be sorted, not the field names (in a database) or column or row headings (in a spreadsheet).

KEY SEQUENCE

From the /Data Sort menu, after positioning the cell pointer in the first cell of the range, type

D *<range>* **Return**

After you press Return, you will be returned to the /Data Sort menu options, where you can go on to define the keys to be used. Because Lotus 1-2-3 remembers the *range* defined with this option, you can perform various sorts on the same range by chaining the primary and secondary keys without redefining the range. When you save the worksheet, the last-defined data range is saved as part of the file.

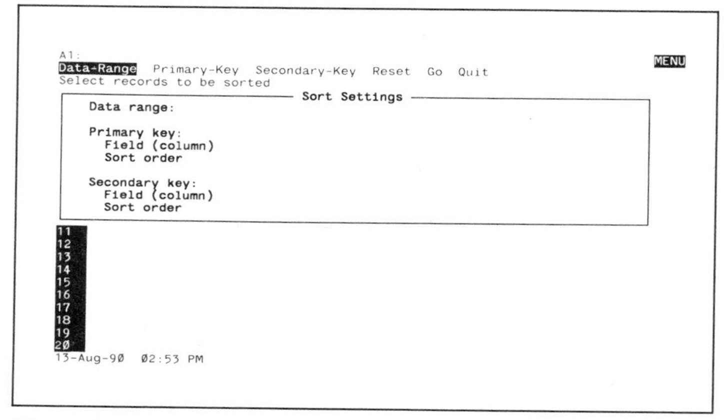

Figure 7.1: The Sort settings sheet

Primary Key

The Primary-Key option indicates the field or column that is to be used first in determining the new order of the records or data specified with the Data-Range option.

KEY SEQUENCE

From the /Data Sort menu, type

P *<column>* **Return** *<A/D>* **Return**

You can indicate the *column* that contains the data by which the sort is to be performed by pointing or by typing in an appropriate cell address. This can be a cell address in any row of this column (even outside the rows in the data range).

You will then be prompted to indicate the type of sort: either **A** for ascending order or **D** for descending order. The first time you define a primary key, Lotus 1-2-3 will supply D as the default sort order. After that, it will use whatever sort order was used previously.

After you type A or D and press Return, you will be returned to the /Data Sort menu options, where you can either indicate a secondary key with the Secondary-Key option or have the program perform the sorting operation by using the Go option.

Secondary Key

The Secondary-Key option defines a second field or column of data to be used in determining the arrangement of records that contain duplicate entries in the primary key field. It is defined in exactly the same way as the primary key.

KEY SEQUENCE

From the /Data Sort menu, type

S *<column>* **Return** *<A/D>* **Return**

Reset

This option clears the ranges set with the Data-Range, Primary-Key, and Secondary-Key options. Because Lotus 1-2-3 remembers all of these ranges throughout a work session, the Reset option is often used when you are about to sort a completely different data range on totally new keys.

KEY SEQUENCE

From the /Data Sort menu, type

R

Go

This option tells the program to go ahead and perform the sort according to the definitions set up with the Data-Range, Primary-Key, and Secondary-Key options.

KEY SEQUENCE

From the /Data Sort menu, type

G

Once you type **G** for Go, the program begins rearranging the data or records in the data range. To abort a sort operation before the program has finished sorting, type **Q** for Quit (or press Ctrl-Scroll Lock, also called the Break key combination).

Quit

The Quit option is used to return to READY mode. It provides a faster alternative for bailing out of a sort operation than pressing the Break key combination. It is also an easier method of exiting from the /Data Sort menu than pressing the Esc key several times.

KEY SEQUENCE

From the /Data Sort menu, type

Q

/DQ

The /Data Query Command

The /Data Query commands are used to locate all records in the database that match the criteria you set up. These search criteria are entered into cells of the same worksheet as that containing the database.

KEY SEQUENCE

/DQ *<option>*

When you press **/DQ**, the Query settings sheet (illustrated in Figure 7.2) appears, showing the current cell addresses of the input, criteria, and output ranges, and a menu.

OPTIONS

- Input: defines input range.
- Criteria: defines criteria range.
- Output: defines output range.
- Find: highlights all records that meet your criteria.
- Extract: copies all of the records that meet your criteria into a new area of the worksheet.
- Unique: works just like an Extract operation except that it copies only unique records, eliminating any complete duplicates.

- Delete: eliminates records that meet your criteria from the database.
- Reset: clears currently defined input, criterion, and ouput ranges.
- Quit: puts the program directly into READY mode.

As with other /Data command menus, after using a particular option you are returned to the /Data Query menu rather than to READY mode. Therefore, to make it easier to return to READY mode, the menu includes a Quit command as one of its options.

Input

The input range defined with the Input option consists of the cell range containing the field names as well as all cells containing records in the database. It must be defined before any /Data Query operation can be performed.

KEY SEQUENCE

From the /Data Query menu, type

I *<range>* **Return**

You can indicate the *range* containing the database field names and records by typing in the cell addresses or range name or by using the pointing method.

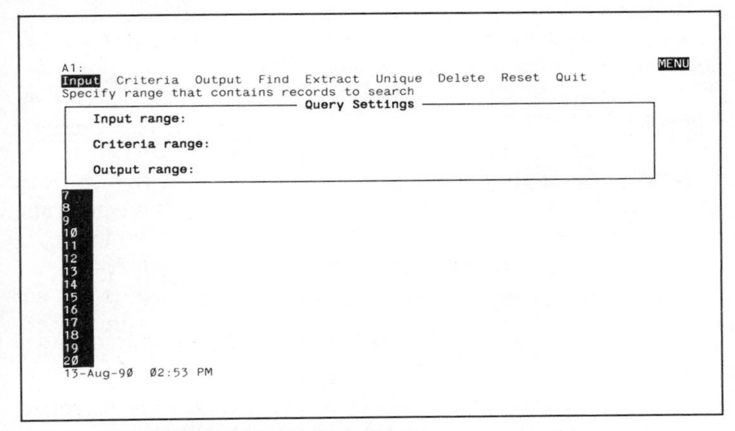

Figure 7.2: The Query settings sheet

Criteria

The criteria range must contain at least one of the field names found in the first row of the database and at least a single cell located directly beneath it. The cell beneath the field name is where you enter the criterion that the program uses to locate matching records.

KEY SEQUENCE

From the /Data Query menu, type

C *<range>* **Return**

Indicate the *range* of cells containing the field names and criteria input cells by typing the cell addresses or range name or by pointing to them. The criteria range should be positioned in an area of the worksheet where it cannot overlap either the input or output ranges.

Setting Up Conditions

To set up AND conditions using exact-match criteria, enter the values or labels to be matched under the appropriate field names in the criteria range. To set up OR conditions using exact-match criteria, enter the values or labels to be matched in separate rows below the appropriate field names. When you set up such OR conditions, you must also make sure that these entries are included as part of the criteria range.

You can also set up criterion formulas with search criteria that contain ranges of values between which matching records must fall. These formulas can contain logical and Boolean operators, as well as Lotus 1-2-3 functions.

When you set up such formulas, you enter cell references that correspond to the appropriate field in the first record of the database where the criterion is to apply. This cell reference tells the program which field to search (rather than using the field name to locate it) and ensures that all records in the database will be included in the search. If the condition set up in the criterion formula is true in the case of this first field entry, the program returns a 1 in the cell where the formula was entered. If it is not, the program returns 0 in this cell.

Output

The output range tells the program where to copy records that meet the search criteria defined in the criterion range when either a /Data Query Extract or Unique command is issued.

KEY SEQUENCE

From the /Data Query menu, type

O *<range>*

Indicate the cell addresses of all the field names you want to use by typing them in or pointing to them. At a minimum, the output *range* can consist of the row of field names copied from the database that indicate which fields of the matching records are to be copied into the output range. If the output range consists of the single row of cells containing these field names, Lotus 1-2-3 will use all rows it requires directly below them to copy the records that meet the search criteria.

Restricting the Output Range

You can also restrict the output range to a cell range including a specific number of blank rows below the field names as well as each of the field names to be used. If more records match the search criteria in an extract operation than will fit in this limited number of rows, Lotus 1-2-3 will copy as many as it can, go into ERROR mode, and display the error message *Too many records for Output range.* You will then have to redefine the extent of the output range and perform your extract operation a second time.

When you enter the field names to be included in the output range, you can include only the names of those fields you want to be displayed in the extracted report, and you can arrange them in any order you want. The only restriction on setting up field names in the output range is that they must be spelled as they are in the input range (though there may be case differences).

Find

This command highlights all records that meet the search criteria entered into the criterion range.

KEY SEQUENCE

From the /Data Query menu, type

F

Lotus 1-2-3 highlights all fields in the first record that meets the criteria. To see whether other records in the database have been located, press the ↓ key. You can continue to view all of the matches in this way. When you press the ↓ key after Lotus 1-2-3 has reached the last matching record, the program beeps to indicate that it has highlighted the last match.

When you perform a Find operation with this command, the program enters FIND mode to let you know that the search is currently under way. When in this mode, you can press the ↑ key to return to the previously highlighted record. You can also stop and edit a record's contents while in FIND mode. To edit a field entry, use the Edit key (F2).

To exit from FIND mode and return to READY mode, press Return. If you have just finished performing a Find operation and quit the /Data Query menu, you can perform another Find operation by pressing the Query key (F7) instead of having to type **/DQF**.

Extract

The Extract operation copies the contents of the fields in records that match the search criteria in the criterion range below the appropriate field names included in the output range. You cannot issue this command without having first defined an output range in addition to an input and criterion range.

KEY SEQUENCE

From the /Data Query menu, after entering the criteria on which the records are to be extracted, type

E

If the last /Data Query operation you performed was an Extract operation, you can perform another by changing the criteria in the criterion range and then pressing the Query key (F7). Lotus 1-2-3 will clear the output range of any data placed there during the last Extract operation before copying all records that meet the new criteria. If you want to save the results of a previous /Data Query operation, you must move the data in the output range to a new location in the worksheet, save it in a new file with the /File Xtract command, or define a new output range to prevent the data from being overwritten by the next extraction.

Unique

This option works like the Extract option, except that it copies only unique records that meet the specified criteria to the output range.

Because duplicate records are eliminated, you can use this command to purge a database of any identical records you may have added by mistake. For two records to qualify as duplicates, all entries in each of their fields must be the same. The /Data Query Unique command can also be used to view the unique entries in a particular field of the database.

KEY SEQUENCE

From the /Data Query menu, after entering criteria, type

U

Delete

This option is used to delete records in the database that match the search criteria set up in the criterion range at the time the command is issued.

KEY SEQUENCE

From the /Data Query menu, type

D *<D/C>*

Choose **D** for Delete to have Lotus 1-2-3 go ahead and delete all matching records. Choose **C** for Cancel if you wish to abort the Delete command, especially if you realize at that point that you have not yet saved a copy of the current database.

Reset

This option clears the currently defined input, criterion, and output ranges.

KEY SEQUENCE

From the /Data Query menu, type

R

All three ranges will be cleared immediately. If you save the worksheet immediately after using this command, none of these ranges will be defined when you retrieve the worksheet.

Quit

This command puts the program directly into READY mode. It can be used to abort an Extract operation quickly without requiring you to press the Esc key repeatedly or use the Break key combination (Ctrl-Scroll Lock). It also allows you to return to the worksheet, where you can define new criteria to be used in further Find, Extract, or Delete operations.

KEY SEQUENCE

From the /Data Query menu, type

Q

/DD

The /Data Distribution Command

This command determines the frequency with which values in a range fall within specified intervals or *bins.*

KEY SEQUENCE

/DD *<values range>* **Return** *<bin range>* **Return**

You must specify two cell ranges: a *values range* containing all of the data to be classified and a *bin range* containing the maximum value for each classification. The values range should not contain any blank columns or rows within it. Such empty areas will affect the results obtained with this command. Also, make sure that the values range does not contain any NA or ERR values within it. These are counted in the frequency statistics, as are empty cells.

When setting up a bin range in the worksheet, you must arrange your interval values in ascending order. If necessary, use the /Data Sort command to arrange them in order. If all the intervals in the range are equal, you can use /Data Fill to create the values.

The cells in the column immediately to the right of the bin range must be blank. This is the area Lotus 1-2-3 automatically uses as the output range, into which the frequency distribution results are placed. This range must also contain one empty cell at the bottom, in which the number of values exceeding the last interval value in the bin range is placed. Any data that exists in this range before using the /Data Distribution command will be overwritten by the data it generates.

SEE ALSO

/Data Fill
/Data Sort

/DM

The /Data Matrix Command

This command provides you with the means to perform matrix inversion and multiplication. A matrix is described first by the number of the rows and then by the number of columns within it. A matrix's size is the number of rows it occupies by the number of columns; a matrix that takes up four rows and three columns in a spreadsheet is called a 4 × 3 matrix. A 90 × 90 matrix is the largest possible matrix that can be used with either /Data Matrix command.

OPTIONS

- Invert
- Multiply

Invert

You can invert only a square matrix (one in which the numbers of rows and columns are equal). For example, if you tried to use the

/Data Matrix Invert command on a 4 × 3 matrix, Lotus 1-2-3 would go into ERROR mode and display the error message *Not a square matrix.*

KEY SEQUENCE

/DMI *<invert range>* **Return** *<output range>* **Return**

The program first prompts you to indicate the cell *range* that contains the matrix to be *inverted.* You can indicate it by typing the addresses of the cells, entering a range name, or pointing out the range with the cell pointer. Next, the program prompts you to indicate the *output* cell *range* where Lotus 1-2-3 will locate the inverted values. You can indicate the first cell of this range either by cell address or by pointing to it. After you press Return, the program will calculate the inverted values.

NOTE

Certain matrices are singular, meaning that their values cannot be inverted. If the values in your matrix cannot be inverted, the program will let you know by displaying the error message *Cannot invert matrix.*

Multiply

To multiply two matrices, the number of columns in the first matrix must equal the number of rows in the second. For example, a 4 × 3 matrix (three columns) can be multiplied only by a second matrix that has three rows. If you tried to multiply a 4 × 3 matrix with one that was 2 × 3, Lotus 1-2-3 would go into ERROR mode and display the error message *Matrices incompatible for multiplication.*

KEY SEQUENCE

/DMM *<first range>* **Return** *<second range>* **Return** *<output range>* **Return**

The program prompts you to specify each cell range. The *first range* to multiply is the location of the cells containing the first matrix. The *second range* to multiply is the location of the cells containing the second matrix. The *output range* marks the cell range where the program will enter the product of this operation. When specifying the output range, you do not need to indicate more than the first cell of this range, although you should make sure that this cell is at the beginning of a sufficiently large blank range that no existing data will be overwritten.

Lotus 1-2-3 always remembers the cell ranges used in a previously issued /Data Matrix Multiply command; it includes no reset option, however. To multiply different matrices in the same worksheet, you must press the Esc key each time to designate the three new cell ranges when using cell pointing.

Adding and Subtracting Matrices

Although the /Data Matrix commands do not include options for adding or subtracting matrices, this can be accomplished by entering one matrix in one worksheet file and the second in another file. Then you can use the /File Combine Add or Subtract commands to perform the required operation. If the matrices you wish to add or subtract are located in the same worksheet, use the /File Xtract command to copy one of them into a separate file before using the appropriate /File Combine command.

/DR

The /Data Regression Command

This command provides you with the means to perform simple or multiple linear regression analysis. Simple linear regression involves correlating sample data for the dependent variable with data for a single independent variable. Multiple linear regression involves correlating sample data for the dependent variable with data for up to 16 independent variables.

The /Data Regression commands are used to obtain statistics that indicate the strength of the relationship between two or more sets of data in a worksheet. If a strong relationship or high correlation is shown to exist between them, these statistics can be used to predict future trends and returns.

Performing Regression Analysis

To perform regression analysis, you must have at least two paired sets of data, one representing the dependent variable and another representing the independent variable. The dependent variable contains the predicted values and is designated as the Y variable. The independent variable contains the known values and is designated as the X variable. If the data in these variables is shown to be strongly related, a change in the X variable will predict the amount of change in the Y variable.

Whenever you use the /Data Regression command, Lotus 1-2-3 returns a standard set of specific regression statistics in an area of the worksheet indicated as the output range. These statistics are listed as follows:

- Constant: the value of the Y intercept of the estimated regression line.
- Std Err of Y Est: the average of the differences between the estimated values on the regression line and the observed values of the dependent variable.
- R Squared: the coefficient of determination, which gives you an idea of the strength of the relationship between the variables.
- No. of Observations: the number of values in the sample data.
- Degrees of Freedom: 2 less than the number of observations (N−2).
- X Coefficient(s): the slope of the estimated regression line (or lines, if multiple regression analysis involving several independent variables has been performed).
- Std Err of Coef.: the average difference between the X coefficient of the estimated regression line and that of the independent variable.

Using the /Data Regression Command

The /Data Regression command options are arranged in a menu much like the one associated with the /Print command. On it, you can define various parameters before using the Go option to have the program perform the regression analysis. However, unlike the /Print command, the /Data Regression command does not include a Quit option to return to READY mode. Instead, you are automatically returned to READY mode as soon as the calculations are complete and Lotus 1-2-3 has created the regression output table in the worksheet.

KEY SEQUENCE

/DR *<X-Range>* **Return** *<Y-Range>* **Return** *<Output-Range>* **Return** *<options>* **G**

When you press **/DR**, the Regression settings sheet (illustrated in Figure 7.3) appears, showing the addresses of the X, Y, and output ranges and of the Y intercept. By default, the intercept is computed automatically.

OPTIONS

- X-Range: cell range containing independent variable values.
- Y-Range: cell range containing dependent variable values.
- Output-Range: where the program places the regression output table.
- Intercept Compute
- Intercept Zero
- Reset
- Go
- Quit

To use the /Data Regression command, you must specify three cell ranges: the X-range, the Y-range, and the Output-Range. You

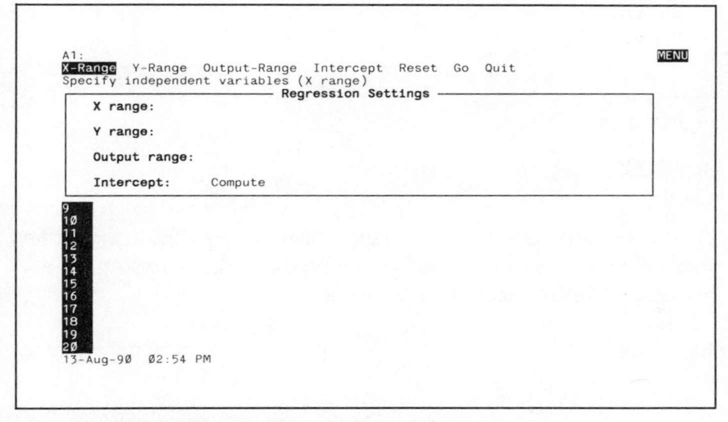

Figure 7.3: The Regression settings sheet

can indicate each cell *range* by typing in the cell addresses, entering a range name, or pointing to it. The Output-Range must be located in an area of the worksheet that contains a sufficiently large area of blank cells to accommodate this table without destroying existing data. Such a table requires nine rows of the spreadsheet and two more columns than the number of columns used to indicate the Y- and X-ranges. When you indicate this range, you need only indicate the cell address or point to the location of the first cell in it.

When entering your sample data, organize the dependent variable in one column of the worksheet. When using more than one independent variable, you must arrange the values in a contiguous cell range with each column containing the values for each independent variable. The number of rows in each range must be the same, because regression analysis requires the use of paired data variables.

After defining the X and Y ranges, you can type **G** to have the program perform the necessary calculations. If you do, Lotus 1-2-3 will use the Compute default to compute the Y intercept for the estimated regression line. If you wish, you can force it to use zero as the Y intercept point by typing **IZ** (for Intercept Zero) before using the Go option. To reset the program to the Compute default later, type **IC**.

Lotus 1-2-3 will remember the options defined from the /Data Regression command menu during a work session and will save them in the worksheet file when you next use the /File Save command. If you wish to perform regression analysis using new data variables in the worksheet, you can use the Reset option to clear the previously used variables and settings. This makes it a lot easier to define new X and Y ranges if you are doing this by pointing.

/DP

The /Data Parse Command

This command allows you to create format lines that instruct the program where to split up individual items in a cell label into separate cell entries in succeeding columns.

KEY SEQUENCE

/DP *<option>*

When you press **/DP**, the Parse settings sheet (illustrated in Figure 7.4) appears, showing the input column and output range addresses and a menu.

OPTIONS

- Format-Line Create
- Format-Line Edit
- Input-Column
- Output-Range
- Go
- Reset
- Quit

Format-Line Create

You use the Format-Line Create option to identify each item, the Input-Column option to identify the format lines to be parsed, the Output-Range option to specify where you want the parsed data to begin, and the Go option to have the program perform the parsing operation. In addition, you may want to use the Format-Line Edit option if the program has incorrectly identified your data, or the Reset option to parse labels in a new part of the spreadsheet.

KEY SEQUENCE

After positioning the cell pointer in the first cell containing the labels you want parsed, type

/DPFC

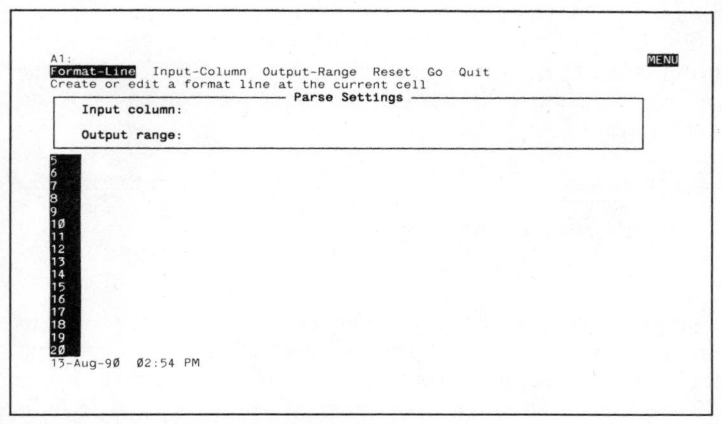

Figure 7.4: The Parse settings sheet

Lotus 1-2-3 will create a format line identifying where each item in the line below begins and its type. You will see one of the following code letters above the first character of each separate item:

- L for Label entry: converts the entries below it into left-aligned labels.
- V for Value entry: converts the entries below it into a right-aligned value that can be used in calculations.
- D for Date entry: converts the entries below it into a date serial number that must be formatted after the parsing is completed.
- T for Time entry: converts the entries below it into a time serial number that must be formatted after the parsing is completed.

Each item, or data block, is separated by at least one space between the characters in the label. The program also places > (greater than) symbols above each subsequent character in this entry and ⋆ (asterisk) symbols to mark all of the unused spaces until the next entry is identified by code letter.

Format-Line Edit

Many times, the data blocks will not be identified correctly in the format line created by Lotus 1-2-3. For example, if you have a column heading that contains a two-word description, the format line will identify each of these as separate entries to be placed in different cells. In such a case, you would edit the format line.

Because the format line is itself a label entry, it can be edited by using either the Format-Line Edit option from the /Data Parse menu or the Edit key (F2) if you use the Quit option on the /Data Parse menu.

KEY SEQUENCE

From the /Data Parse menu, type

FE

This places the cursor on the format line. You can move the cursor to the code letter above the incorrectly identified data block and type the > symbol (used to mark a continuation of a block) over it. When editing a format line this way, the program is in overtype mode, indicated by the OVR status indicator at the bottom of the screen. Once you press Return to have the format line updated, you will also see the CALC indicator immediately to its left. When editing a format line, all of the editing keys work just as they do when you are editing a cell entry.

Changing the Letter Code

When you edit a format line, you can change the type of entry by typing a new letter code over the one entered by Lotus 1-2-3. For instance, to change an item identified as a value (V in the format line) to a label, move the cursor to it and type an **L** over the V. You must be careful when manually editing the codes, because you cannot make an item that begins with a letter or punctuation symbol into a value. If you specify a type that will not work with the data being parsed, the program will go into ERROR mode when you use the Go option from the /Data Parse menu, and you will receive the error message *Invalid format line.*

You can also use the letter **S** as a code to indicate that Lotus 1-2-3 is to skip, or ignore, the item that starts below it. Data blocks below an S will not appear in the cells when the data is parsed. This code can be used whenever you have an entry in the imported data that you do not want to keep in the worksheet.

NOTE

Lotus 1-2-3 can translate entries into date and time serial numbers only if they match one of its date or time formats. If the entries are dates such as 10/31/90, you can convert them into date serial numbers by using the **D** format letter code. However, if they were entered in the form 19901031, they would not be successfully translated into date serial numbers (they would be parsed as labels even if you use the D code).

Leaving the Format Line

Once you have finished making modifications to the format line, press Return to have them updated and to return to the /Data Parse menu. If you wish to leave the format line without having your changes recorded, press the Ctrl-Scroll Lock (Break key) combination. Do not press the Esc key; doing so will erase the entire format line, leaving a blank cell, when the program returns to READY mode. If this happens, you cannot recreate the format line by using the /Data Parse Format-Line Create command without repositioning the cell pointer one cell down from the one that contains the first label to be parsed (the program will not allow you to create a format line in a blank cell).

Using Different Format Lines

You can create as many different format lines as you need to correctly identify the individual items as separate data blocks in subsequent rows of the data. To do so, you must use the /Data Parse Quit (**Q**) option, move the cell pointer to the cell containing the long label that requires different formatting, then access the /Data Parse Format-Line Create command again by typing **/DPFC**. Once you have created other format lines, you can edit them, if required, just as you did the original one.

Input-Column

Once you have created and edited all of the format lines that are required to mark all of the separate data blocks, use the Input-Column option to identify the cell range containing both the format lines and the data to be parsed.

KEY SEQUENCE

From the /Data Parse menu, type

I *<range>* **Return**

Indicate the *range* by typing the cell addresses or by pointing.

The input range must contain the format lines that have been created as well as all of the data below each one. (Because each format line is entered in this new row as a special long label entry (prefaced by | in the literal contents of the cell), the format lines all exist in a single column of the worksheet, and your input range will always be a cell range only one column wide.) If you do not begin this range with the first format line, the program will go into ERROR mode when you use the Go option from the /Data Parse menu, and you will receive the error message *Parse input must start with format lines.*

Output-Range

Next, indicate the location of the output range.

KEY SEQUENCE

From the /Data Parse menu, type

O *<range>* **Return**

For the *range*, you need indicate only the first cell where you want the parsed data to begin. Lotus 1-2-3 will use whatever columns and rows are required from that cell on when parsing the data into individual cells. Thus, make sure that there is no existing data in the vicinity that could be destroyed when you give the go-ahead to have the program parse your labels.

Go

After indicating the output range and typing Return, access the Go option to have the parsing operation performed.

KEY SEQUENCE

From the /Data Parse menu, type

G

Once the data has been copied into separate cells, you may erase the original label entries and format lines from the worksheet using the /Range Erase command. If you wish, you can then move the newly parsed data to another place in the worksheet.

Reset

If you find that your data is not correctly parsed and you wish to use the same output range when you redo the command, first erase the existing data. The /Data Parse Reset option will clear both the previously set input and output ranges. Use it if you need to parse labels in a new part of the spreadsheet during the current work session.

KEY SEQUENCE

From the /Data Parse menu, type

R

8

The /System, /Add-In, and /Quit Commands

The /System command temporarily suspends the Lotus 1-2-3 work session and exits to DOS, where you can use almost any DOS command (such as CD, MD, RD, DIR, FORMAT, CHKDSK, and DEL). You cannot use the so-called Terminate and Stay Resident (TSR) DOS commands, such as PRINT, GRAPHICS, and MODE. You can also start other software application programs (if your computer has sufficient memory). During this time, the Lotus 1-2-3 program and the worksheet you are working on remain in the computer's memory.

The /Add-In command allows you to attach, detach, and invoke add-in programs such as Allways and the Macro Library Manager (both of which come with 1-2-3) as well as many other popular programs.

The /Quit command terminates your session with Lotus 1-2-3. It allows you to leave Lotus 1-2-3. If you used **123** as the start-up command, you will be returned to DOS. If you started by entering **LOTUS**, you will be returned to the main Lotus Access menu, from which you can use the PrintGraph, Install, and Translate programs or select the Exit option to return to DOS.

/S

The /System Command

KEY SEQUENCE

/S

You are immediately placed in the DOS directory containing the Lotus 1-2-3 program files (A:\ on a two-drive system, and C:\LOTUS, C:\123, etc., on a hard disk system). The program also displays the message

(Type EXIT and press ENTER to return to 1-2-3)

If you are using Lotus 1-2-3 on a two-drive system and have not copied the COMMAND.COM file onto your Lotus System Disk, you will receive the error message *Cannot invoke DOS.* In such a case, replace your Lotus System Disk with a copy of your DOS disk and then press the Esc key to complete the command. To return to the Lotus 1-2-3 worksheet and continue your work, type **EXIT** and press Return (you can do this from any DOS directory).

Using Other Programs

The warning about not using TSR DOS commands also extends to starting up any other programs that terminate and stay resident, such as SideKick or SuperKey. The only programs that you can safely load are those like WordPerfect or dBASE, which are erased from memory when you exit from them. In addition, using these programs is possible only if your computer has sufficient memory to hold Lotus 1-2-3, the worksheet you were working on before using the /System command, and the new program files.

Returning to the Program

Unlike other programs that provide a DOS shell command (such as WordPerfect, which continues to display its *Type Exit* message after every DOS command you use), Lotus 1-2-3 will not continue to display this message to remind you that you have exited to DOS. You may forget that you have exited to DOS and try to load a TSR program or use a TSR command. You may even forget that you need to type **EXIT** to return to Lotus 1-2-3. It is up to you to remember that you have made a temporary exit from the program.

Saving Your Worksheet

As a precaution against losing data, always save the worksheet currently loaded in memory before you use the /System command. If you execute the /System command in error, for example, when meaning to save the file with the /File Save command, immediately type **EXIT** to return to the worksheet and issue the save command as intended.

SEE ALSO

/Quit

/A

2.2

The /Add-In Command

KEY SEQUENCE

/A *<A/D/I/C>* *<Add-In>* **Return**

OPTIONS

- Attach: brings an add-in into the computer's memory and tells Lotus how you want to start it.
- Detach: removes an add-in from memory that has already been attached.
- Invoke: executes an add-in that has already been attached.
- Clear: removes all attached add-ins from memory.

NOTE

Once you attach an Add-In @function, you cannot remove it from memory with either /Add-In Detach or /Add-In Clear. However, the function will not remain in memory after you exit and restart Lotus 1-2-3 unless you configured it, with the /Worksheet Global Default Other Add-In command, to attach automatically when 1-2-3 starts.

The /Add-In Attach Command

KEY SEQUENCE

/AA *<Add-In>* **Return** *<N/7/8/9/1>*

When you use /Add-In Attach, you are presented with a list of available add-ins as well as any directories that might contain add-ins. Select one of the add-ins (or a directory and then an add-in) and you will see the following options:

OPTIONS

- No-Key: sets up an add-in, so that you need to enter **/AI** *<Add-In>* to run it.
- 7: assigns the add-in to the Alt-F7 key.
- 8: assigns the add-in to the Alt-F8 key.
- 9: assigns the add-in to the Alt-F9 key.
- 1(0): assigns the add-in to the Alt-F10 key.

With options 1–7, you can also use the Shift key to invoke the add-in; for example, Shift-F7 to run an add-in assigned to Alt-F7.

NOTE

After one of the Alt-function key combinations has been defined, it doesn't appear in this menu again until it is detached or you restart Lotus 1-2-3.

SEE ALSO

/Worksheet Global Default Other Add-In

/Q

The /Quit Command

KEY SEQUENCE

/Q *<Y/N>* **[***<Y/N>***]**

Choose **N** for No, the default, or press Return if you entered the /Quit command by mistake or realize that you are exiting from the program without having first saved the worksheet currently in memory. You will return immediately to the worksheet. To go ahead and exit from Lotus 1-2-3, type **Y** for Yes; if you started Lotus 1-2-3 by typing **123**, you will be returned to DOS. If you entered **LOTUS** as the start-up command, you will be returned to the Lotus Access System Menu.

Release 2.2 has added an extra precaution to this process. If you changed the worksheet but didn't save it before selecting the Quit option, 1-2-3 will beep and tell you so. It will then ask if you really want to exit without saving the changes. This feature could save you a lot of time and frustration.

Using Other Programs

Unlike the /System command, once you have reentered DOS with the /Quit command, you are free to start up other programs and use the DOS commands that terminate and stay resident.

Protecting Your Data

If you have already saved your work, you can power down your computer without using the /Quit Yes command and not cause damage to either the program or your data. However, this is not the preferred method for terminating a work session, because the habit of turning off the power without bothering to use the /Quit command can lead you to use this method with other programs that do require an exit to prevent data corruption (as do most stand-alone database-management programs).

SEE ALSO

/System

9

Mathematical Functions

The mathematical functions include two types: those that calculate new values—such as @MOD, @RAND, and @SQRT—and those that alter the way Lotus 1-2-3 stores values already calculated—such as @ABS, @INT, and @ROUND.

@ABS

The Absolute Value Function

The @ABS function returns the absolute value of an expression; that is, its value without regard to a positive or negative sign.

SYNTAX

@ABS(*x*)

where *x* is a value input into a cell, a cell reference to a value, or a value derived by formula calculation.

USAGE

This function is most often used to ensure that the value returned is not negative, because the absolute value of any number is equivalent to its positive value.

EXAMPLE

Entering either

@ABS(45)

or

@ABS(– 45)

returns a value of 45 in the cell in which this function was entered.

NOTES

The @ABS function in Lotus 1-2-3 can be used only with single values. It will not accept a cell range as its argument. If you need to use only the absolute value of cells in a given range, you have to enter the @ABS function for each cell in that range.

@INT

The Integer Function

The @INT function returns the integer part of a value by stripping away any values following the decimal point.

SYNTAX

@INT(*x*)

where *x* is a value input into a cell, a cell reference to a value, or a value derived by formula calculation.

USAGE

The @INT function truncates numbers so that only the integer portion of the value is used in further calculations. The value can be positive or negative. This function does not round the value; it merely truncates it by removing all decimal values.

EXAMPLE

Entering

@INT(– 34.56)

in a cell returns – 34 as the value in that cell.

@MOD

The Modulus Function

The @MOD function returns the remainder after division of two numbers specified as the arguments of the function. This remainder is referred to in mathematics as the *modulus,* thus the name @MOD.

SYNTAX

@MOD(*x*,*y*)

where *x* is the dividend and *y* is the divisor. In using @MOD, *x* and *y* can be values input into cells or values derived by formula calculation.

USAGE

This function takes two arguments, the first of which, *x*, is divided by the second, *y*. It can be used to test whether a cell contains an even or odd value as well as in any situation that calls for using the remainder in calculations.

EXAMPLE

Entering

@MOD(C4,2)

in a cell, when C4 contains the value 5, returns 1 (the remainder of dividing 5 by 2) in that cell.

@RAND

The Random Number Function

The @RAND function generates a random number between 0 and 1.

SYNTAX

@RAND

The @RAND function takes no argument. It is merely entered into a cell or combined within another Lotus 1-2-3 function.

USAGE

The @RAND function returns a value between 0 and 1 with a precision of 15 decimal places. The value it returns is recalculated each time the spreadsheet is recalculated, either when you press the Calc key (F9) if the program is in manual recalculation mode or when you enter a new value if the spreadsheet is in automatic mode.

To prevent @RAND from recalculating a new number, you must convert the value returned by @RAND to a constant value by using the /Range Value command.

NOTE

If you use @RAND by itself, the value will be a decimal number between 0 and less than 1. To generate numbers within a specific range, multiply the @RAND function by the difference between the upper and lower limits and add the number of the lower limit to the result. To obtain a whole random number, you can use either the @ROUND function or the @INT function.

@ROUND

The Round Function

The @ROUND function rounds a value to the place value specified in the arguments.

SYNTAX

@ROUND(*x*,*n*)

where *x* is a value input into a cell, a cell reference to a value, or a value derived by formula calculation, and *n* is the number of digits to be rounded.

USAGE

The *n* argument can be a number between −15 and 15, specifying the amount and placement of digits to be affected. If *n* is a negative number, the program rounds to the left of the *x* value's decimal point to the number of digits specified. If *n* is positive, the program rounds to the right of the *x* value's decimal point to the number of digits specified. If *n* is zero, the program rounds the *x* value to the nearest integer.

EXAMPLES

If you enter

@ROUND(15675.3456,0)

in a cell, Lotus 1-2-3 returns 15675. If you modify the function to

@ROUND(15675.3456,1)

in the cell, Lotus 1-2-3 returns 15675.3 (.3456 is rounded to .3). If you modify the function to

@ROUND(15675.3456 – 1)

in the cell, Lotus 1-2-3 returns 15680 (75 is rounded to 80).

@SQRT

The Square Root Function

The @SQRT function returns the square root of a positive value.

SYNTAX

@SQRT(*x*)

where *x* is a positive value input into a cell, a cell reference to a value, or a value derived by formula calculation. Lotus 1-2-3 returns an ERR value if the value is negative.

USAGE

The @SQRT function can find the square root only of positive values in the spreadsheet. Because it will return an ERR value if the value is negative, you can combine it with the @ABS function if you know that the value will be negative or if you are not sure and want to guard against error values. To do this, use the following paradigm:

@SQRT(@ABS(*x*))

EXAMPLE

Entering

@SQRT(B2)

in a cell, when B2 contains the value 1600, returns the value of 40. If B2 contained the value −1600, it would return the ERR value. To avoid this error value, you would enter

@SQRT(@ABS(B2))

10

Scientific Functions

Lotus 1-2-3 includes several powerful functions that are most often required in scientific and engineering worksheet applications. The program supports logarithmic functions in two bases: the natural logarithm in base **e** with @LN and its inverse, @EXP, as well as logarithms in base 10 with @LOG.

In addition to logarithms, Lotus 1-2-3 has a variety of trigonometric functions. These include @PI to return the value of π, as well as the three basic trig functions: @SIN to return the sine of the angle, @COS to return its cosine, and @TAN to return its tangent. Lotus 1-2-3 also includes the inverse functions of sine, cosine, and tangent in @ASIN for arcsine, @ACOS for arccosine, @ATAN for arctangent, and @ATAN2, which allows you to derive the arctangent in a four-quadrant system.

@ACOS

The Arccosine Function

The @ACOS function returns the arccosine, an angle measured in radians, from the cosine specified as its argument. To convert from radians to degrees, multiply the value returned by 180/@PI.

SYNTAX

@ACOS(*x*)

where *x* is the cosine of the angle to be solved for. The *x* argument can be a value input in the function, referenced by cell address, or calculated by formula. It must be between −1 and 1; otherwise, the program will return an ERR value.

EXAMPLE

In a right triangle where you know that the adjacent side of the triangle measures 12 feet and the hypotenuse measures 13 feet, you can determine angle θ by using the @ACOS function as follows:

@ACOS(12/13)*180/@PI

Lotus 1-2-3 returns 22.61986; the angle is approximately 22.62 degrees.

@ASIN

The Arcsine Function

The @ASIN function returns the arcsine, an angle measured in radians, from the sine specified as its argument. To convert from radians to degrees, multiply the value returned by 180/@PI.

SYNTAX

@ASIN(*x*)

where x is the sine of the angle to be solved for. The x argument can be a value input in the function, referenced by cell address, or calculated by formula. It must be between −1 and 1; otherwise, the program will return an ERR value.

EXAMPLE

In a right triangle where you know that the opposite side of the triangle measures 5 feet and the hypotenuse measures 13 feet, you can determine angle θ by using the @ASIN function as follows:

@ASIN(5/13)*180/@PI

Lotus 1-2-3 returns 22.61986; the angle is approximately 22.62 degrees.

@ATAN

The Arctangent Function

The @ATAN function returns the arctangent, an angle measured in radians, from the tangent specified as its argument. To convert from radians to degrees, multiply the value returned by 180/@PI.

SYNTAX

ATAN(*x*)

where *x* is the tangent of the angle to be solved for. The *x* argument can be a value input in the function, referenced by cell address, or calculated by formula.

EXAMPLE

In a right triangle where you know that the opposite side of the triangle measures 5 feet and the adjacent side measures 12 feet, you can determine angle θ by using the @ATAN function as follows:

@ATAN(5/12)*180/@PI

Lotus 1-2-3 returns 22.61986; the angle is approximately 22.62 degrees.

@ATAN2

The Four-Quadrant Arctangent Function

The @ATAN2 function returns the four-quadrant arctangent, an angle measured in radians, from the values for *x* and *y* specified as its arguments.

SYNTAX

@ATAN2(*x*,*y*)

where *x* and *y* are numeric values input into the function, referenced by cell address, or calculated by formula.

USAGE

The @ATAN2 function allows you to calculate the value of the arctangent by specifying the x and y coordinates in a four-quadrant system instead of using the value of the tangent, as with @ATAN. The result returned by the program will be between $-\pi$ and π. If you specify both x and y as 0, Lotus 1-2-3 returns an ERR value.

The formula for deriving the arctangent is y/x, where x is not equal to 0. To derive the arctangent, you specify the values of x and y separated by a comma as arguments of the function. The range of values that will be returned by the function depends on the sign (and thus the quadrant) of x and y.

EXAMPLE

In a right triangle where you know that the opposite side of the triangle measures 5 feet and the adjacent side measures 12 feet, you can determine angle θ by using the @ATAN2 function as follows:

@ATAN2(12,5)*180/@PI

Lotus 1-2-3 returns 22.61986; the angle is approximately 22.62 degrees.

@COS

The Cosine Function

The @COS function returns the cosine of the angle specified as its argument expressed in radians. It is most useful in scientific and engineering formulas that involve right triangles and their various relationships. To convert an angle measured in degrees into radians for use with this function, multiply the number of degrees by @PI/180. To use the secant function in your formulas, use the reciprocal of the @COS function in Lotus 1-2-3.

SYNTAX

@COS(*x*)

where x is a measurement of the angle expressed in radians.

EXAMPLE

The values returned by this function vary between -1 and 1, which is suggested by the following relationship:

- If $\theta = 0^r$ (0°) then $\cos \theta = 1$
- If $\theta = \pi^r/2$ (90°) then $\cos \theta = 0$

In Lotus 1-2-3, you can verify this by entering the following formulas:

@COS(0)

@COS(@PI/2)

The results are 1 and 3.4E–19 (approximating 0), respectively.

@EXP

The Exponent Function

The @EXP function returns the value of the constant **e** raised to the power specified as the argument of the function. It represents the inverse of the Lotus 1-2-3 function @LN.

SYNTAX

@EXP(*x*)

where *x* is a value input into a cell, a cell reference to such a value, or a value calculated by formula.

USAGE

The @EXP function uses the constant **e**, which is approximately equal to 2.7182818. This represents the constant of base **e** used in natural logarithms. The *x* argument that you supply in the function represents the exponent or power by which the constant **e** is raised in calculation.

EXAMPLES

Radioactive materials are known to decay spontaneously at a rate that depends on the amount of material present at any given time.

The amount decreases exponentially depending on the half-life of the material. In the case of strontium 90, you can calculate the approximate amount of remaining material by the formula

$$M = G\mathbf{e}^{-.0248t}$$

where M is the amount of strontium 90 remaining, G is the number of grams of material you start with, and t is the number of years. To find the amount of strontium 90 remaining after 80 years when you start with 10 grams, enter the formula as follows:

@EXP(−0.0248*80)*10

As you can see, you supply the exponent of **e** as the argument of the function within the parentheses. In this case, it is the calculated value of -0.0248×80, which is then multiplied by the number of grams you started with. Lotus 1-2-3 then tells you that 1.375180, or approximately 1.38, grams of the original 10 grams of strontium 90 remain after 80 years have passed.

To use the constant **e** in other formulas, you can use the @EXP function to generate its value. In this case, using the number 1 as the argument results in the value of **e**, as follows:

@EXP(1) = 2.7182818285

@LOG

The Logarithm Function

The @LOG function is the reciprocal of base-10 exponentiation, or scientific notation. It returns the logarithm of its argument. It solves for the logarithm of the argument to the base 10.

SYNTAX

@LOG(*x*)

where x is a value input into a cell, a cell reference to such a value, or a value calculated by formula. If the value is negative or equal to zero, the program will return an ERR value.

EXAMPLES

The decibel rating of an event can be calculated by the formula

$$L = 10 \log_{10} \frac{I}{I_0}$$

where L is the decibel rating, I is the sound intensity, and I_0 is the threshold intensity of human hearing. To find the decibel rating of a jet plane on takeoff if its sound intensity is rated as $10^{12} I_0$, enter the formula

@LOG(10^12)*10

Lotus 1-2-3 returns a sound intensity level at takeoff of 120 decibels.

To find logarithms in other bases with the @LOG function, divide the number whose logarithm you wish to find by the base, as in the following example:

@LOG(25)/@LOG(@EXP(1))

The result is 3.2188758249, the logarithm of 25 in base **e**.

@LN

The Natural Log Function

The @LN function is the inverse of @EXP, so the value of @LN(2.7182818285) is 1. It returns the natural logarithm of its argument, solving for the logarithm of the argument to base **e** (the mathematical constant approximately equal to 2.7182818285).

SYNTAX

@LN(*x*)

where x is a value input into a cell, a cell reference to such a value, or a value calculated by formula. If the value is negative or equal to zero, the program returns an ERR value.

EXAMPLE

To determine the approximate number in years for the age of plant or animal remains with carbon 14 dating, use the formula

$$t = \frac{\ln P}{-0.00012}$$

where t is the answer in years and ln is the natural logarithm of P, the percent of radioactive carbon 14 retained by the remains. Thus, to find the age in years of an animal's jawbone that retains 31 percent of its carbon 14, enter the formula as follows:

@LN(0.31)/ – 0.00012

Lotus 1-2-3 returns 9759.85817, showing that the jawbone in question is almost 10,000 years old.

To find logarithms in other bases with the @LN function, divide the number whose logarithm you wish to find by the base, as in the following example:

@LN(25)/@LN(10)

In this example, Lotus 1-2-3 returns the value 1.3979400087, the logarithm of 25 in base 10.

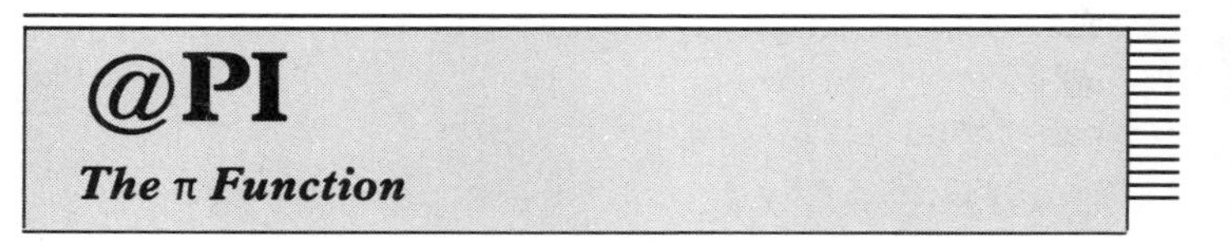

@PI

The π Function

The @PI function returns the value of the constant π, using the value 3.1415926356.

SYNTAX

@PI

The @PI function requires no argument.

EXAMPLE

You can use the @PI function to determine the area of a circle with the standard formula πr^2, as in the following example

@PI*14^2

where 14 inches is the radius of the circle.

The Sine Function

The @SIN function returns the sine of the angle specified as its argument expressed in radians. The answer returned by @SIN function is given in radians and lies between −1 and 1. To convert an angle measured in degrees into radians for use with this function, multiply the number of degrees by @PI/180. To use the cosecant function in your formulas, use the reciprocal of the @SIN function in Lotus 1-2-3.

SYNTAX

@SIN(*x*)

where *x* is a measurement of the angle expressed in radians.

EXAMPLE

To find the index of refraction according to Snell's law for a light ray as it passes from air to another medium, use the formula

$$n = \frac{\sin \theta_i}{\sin \theta_r}$$

where n is the index of refraction for the given medium and θ_i and θ_r are the incident and refracted rays, respectively. To apply this formula to water, which has a θ_i of 43.2 degrees and a θ_r of 31.0 degrees, and find its index of refraction, enter the formula as follows:

@SIN(43.2*@PI/180)/@SIN(31*@PI/180)

Lotus 1-2-3 returns the value 1.329119.

@TAN

The Tangent Function

The @TAN function returns the tangent of the angle specified as its argument expressed in radians. To convert an angle measured in degrees into radians for use with this function, multiply the number of degrees by @PI/180.

SYNTAX

@TAN(*x*)

where x is a measurement of the angle expressed in radians.

USAGE

The range of the values of the tangent is the set of all real numbers, as reflected in the following relationships:

$$\tan\theta \to +\infty \text{ as } \theta \to \frac{\pi}{2}$$

$$\tan\theta \to -\infty \text{ as } \theta \to -\frac{\pi}{2}$$

Lotus 1-2-3 returns the value of ±90° as follows:

@TAN(@PI/2) = 2.9E+18

@TAN(−@PI/2) = −2.9E+18

EXAMPLE

The velocity at which a vehicle can safely travel on a roadway banked at a particular angle can be measured by the formula

$$v = \frac{1800R\tan\theta}{121}$$

where v is the velocity and R is the radius of curvature in feet of the roadway banked at the angle θ. If the angle θ is 6.4 degrees and the radius of curvature is 1460 feet, you can find the velocity with Lotus 1-2-3's @TAN function by constructing the following formula:

@SQRT(1800*1460*@TAN(6.4*@PI/180)/121)

Lotus 1-2-3 returns the value 49.39651. Therefore, a vehicle could travel safely at 49 mph on this roadway under normal driving conditions.

NOTE

To use the cotangent function in your formulas, use the reciprocal of the @TAN function in Lotus 1-2-3.

11

Statistical Functions

The statistical functions—@AVG, @COUNT, @MAX, @MIN, and @SUM—provide you with powerful ways to obtain quantitative data about values in your worksheets. The @STD and @VAR functions have more specialized applications for calculating frequency distributions. Both standard deviation (@STD) and variance (@VAR) use the measurement of the mean to compute how much each individual value in a sample deviates from it.

@AVG

The Average Function

The @AVG function calculates the average (that is, the mean or $\bar{X}$) of the values contained in the list given as its argument.

SYNTAX

@**AVG(***list***)**

where *list* consists of single cells, cell ranges, or a combination of the two, separated by commas. The cells in the list can represent literal values, cell references, or range names. The cell ranges in the list can represent cell references or range names.

USAGE

If the argument list of the @AVG function contains blank cells as well as values, these empty cells have no adverse effect on the correct average of the values. If the list contains labels as well as values, the labels will be counted, thus skewing the average returned. If the list consists of blank cells, the average returned will be ERR.

EXAMPLE

To find the average of the values for the cell range D5..K5 in cell M5, move the cell pointer to cell M5, enter

@AVG(D5..K5)

and press Return.

@COUNT

The Count Function

The @COUNT function counts the nonblank cells contained in the list given as its argument.

SYNTAX

@COUNT(*list*)

where *list* consists of single cells, cell ranges, or a combination of the two, separated by commas.

USAGE

If the argument list of the @COUNT function contains blank cells as well as values, the empty cells have no adverse effect on the correct count of the nonblank cells. If the list contains labels as well as values, the labels will be counted along with all values in the number returned.

EXAMPLE

To obtain a tally of the number of cells in the cell range C5..C47 in cell D2, move the cell pointer to D2, enter

@COUNT(C5..C47)

and press Return.

NOTE

The @COUNT function exhibits an inconsistency when dealing with argument lists that consist of only blank cells. If the list specified contains a range of multiple blank cells, the result obtained from using the @COUNT function is zero. However, if the range consists of a single blank cell, the result obtained is 1.

@MAX

The Maximum Value Function

The @MAX function determines the highest (that is, the maximum) of the values contained in the list given as its argument.

SYNTAX

@MAX(*list*)

where *list* consists of single cells, cell ranges, or a combination of the two, separated by commas. If *list* consists of blank cells, the value returned will be ERR.

EXAMPLE

To enter the highest value in the cell range G10..G84 in cell G2, move the cell pointer to G2, enter

@MAX(G10..G84)

and press Return.

SEE ALSO

@MIN

@MIN

The Minimum Value Function

The @MIN function determines the lowest (that is, the minimum) of the values contained in the list given as its argument.

SYNTAX

@MIN(*list*)

where *list* consists of single cells, cell ranges, or a combination of the two, separated by commas. If *list* contains blank cells or labels as well as values, zero will be returned as the minimum value.

EXAMPLE

To enter the lowest value in the cell range G10..G84 in cell G2, move the cell pointer to G2, enter

@MIN(G10..G84)

and press Return.

SEE ALSO

@MAX

@SUM

The Sum Function

The @SUM function adds all of the values contained in the list given as its argument.

SYNTAX

@SUM(*list*)

where *list* consists of single cells, cell ranges, or a combination of the two, separated by commas. The cells in the list can represent literal values, cell references, or range names. The cell ranges in the list can represent cell references or range names. If *list* contains labels, they do not skew the total, as labels in Lotus 1-2-3 carry a value of zero.

EXAMPLE

To calculate the total of values in the cell range A6..A15 in cell A17, move the cell pointer to cell A17, enter

@SUM(A6..A15)

and press Return.

@STD

The Standard Deviation Function

The @STD function calculates the standard deviation (S) of the values contained in the list given as its argument.

SYNTAX

@STD(*list*)

where *list* consists of single cells, cell ranges, or a combination of the two, separated by commas.

USAGE

Standard deviation measures the degree to which each individual score in a sample varies from the mean of the scores in the sample.

If the argument list of the @STD function contains labels as well as values, the labels will be counted, thus skewing the standard deviation. If the list consists of blank cells, the standard deviation returned will be ERR.

To calculate the degrees of freedom ($N - 1$) in the calculation of the standard deviation, enter the following formula using the @VAR function:

@SQRT(@COUNT(list)/(@COUNT(list) – 1) * @VAR(list))

EXAMPLE

To find the standard deviation in a group of statistics in the cell range A4..A45 in cell A1, move the cell pointer to A1, enter

@STD(A4..A45)

and press Return.

SEE ALSO

@VAR

@VAR

The Variance Function

The @VAR function calculates the variance (S^2) of the values contained in the list given as its argument.

SYNTAX

@VAR(*list*)

where *list* consists of single cells, cell ranges, or a combination of the two, separated by commas.

USAGE

Variance, like standard deviation, measures the degree to which each individual score in a sample varies from the mean of the scores in the sample.

If the argument list of the @VAR function contains labels as well as values, the labels will be counted, thus skewing the variance returned. If the list consists of blank cells, the variance returned will be ERR.

EXAMPLE

To find the variance in a group of statistics in the cell range A4..A45 in cell A1, move the cell pointer to A1, enter

@VAR(A4..A45)

and press Return.

12

Financial Functions

The Lotus 1-2-3 financial functions greatly simplify financial analysis. They take sophisticated formulas for performing calculations concerning present value analysis, investment evaluations, and depreciation and present them as straightforward functions.

@CTERM

The Compound Term Function

The @CTERM function calculates the number of periods (that is, the term) required to realize a particular future value from making an initial investment at a fixed periodic interest rate.

SYNTAX

@CTERM(*int,fv,pv***)**

where *int* is the periodic interest rate, *fv* is the future value of the investment, and *pv* is the present value or initial investment made.

USAGE

The @CTERM function is similar to the @TERM function, except that it determines the number of periods required to achieve a specific future value when you make a single initial deposit or investment instead of a series of payments—thus the difference in arguments between the two functions.

If the interest rate is given as an annual figure, divide it by 12 if it is compounded monthly. To convert the number of periods from months to years, divide the result by 12 also.

EXAMPLE

To determine the term required for doubling an initial investment of $12,000.00 at 10.5 percent interest, enter the following formula:

@CTERM(10.5/12,24000,12000)

Lotus 1-2-3 returns a period of 27.56 months.

@DDB

The Double-Declining Balance Function

The @DDB function calculates the depreciation of an asset using the double-declining balance method for determining accelerated depreciation.

SYNTAX

@DDB(*cost,salvage,life,period*)

where *cost* is the original cost of the asset, *salvage* is the salvage or residual value, *life* is the useful life of the asset, and *period* is the year in which the depreciation is being calculated.

USAGE

Double-declining balance offers a method of determining accelerated depreciation whereby the depreciation percent used in each period is twice the amount. Unlike the sum-of-the-years'-digits method, the double-declining balance method starts with the original cost (rather than the depreciable base), and the final book value of the asset is equal to the salvage value.

EXAMPLE

To calculate the depreciation in the first year using the double-declining method on an item with an original cost of $10,000.00 with a salvage value of $500.00 for a five-year period, enter the following formula:

@DDB(10000,500,5,1)

Lotus 1-2-3 returns $4,000.00 as the amount of depreciation for the first year.

@FV

The Future Value Function

This function calculates the future value of an annuity, given the payment per period and the discount rate over the period of payments specified as the term.

SYNTAX

@FV(*pmt,int,term*)

where *pmt* is the payment per period, *int* is the discount rate, and *term* is the number of payment periods.

USAGE

The @FV function is used to determine the future value, given a series of payments discounted at a periodic interest rate. When you use this function, the period of the interest rate must agree with that of the term.

Also, remember that this function assumes that payments are made at the end of each period in the term specified. To determine an annuity due in which payments are made at the beginning of the period, use this formula:

@FV(*pmt,int,term*)*(1 + *int*)

EXAMPLE

To calculate the future value of an ordinary annuity where the payment is $785.67, the interest rate is 12.5 percent, and the term is 10 years, enter the following formula:

@FV(785.67,12.5,10)

Lotus 1-2-3 returns a value of $15,090.87.

@IRR

The Internal Rate of Return Function

This function calculates the internal rate of return or the discount rate at which the present value of an investment outlay is equal to the present value of annual inflows, or a net present value of zero.

SYNTAX

@IRR(*guess,range*)

where *guess* is an estimated value between 0 and 1, and *range* is the range of values representing the cash flows resulting from the investment.

USAGE

When you use the @IRR function, the anticipated cash flows from the investment can be even or uneven, but it is assumed that they will be received at regular intervals. The first value in the range must be negative.

The internal rate of return can give inconsistent or even misleading indications of the desirability of an investment, especially when the cash flows fluctuate in a series of negative values (as outlays or negative operating inflows other than the initial value in the range) as well as positive values (inflows). Also, the @IRR function assumes that income from the investment is reinvested at the rate of return. When this is not the case, the actual internal rate of return will be less than that indicated by the function.

To arrive at the internal rate of return, you must supply a guess value that represents an estimate of the return rate that you expect to realize. It can be anywhere from 0 (0 percent) to 1 (100 percent). However, you should supply a value that is as realistic as possible (in some cases, you can receive a different internal rate of return as the result of supplying a different guess value).

EXAMPLE

To calculate the internal rate of return for a series of cash flows entered in the cell range B3..G3 using a guess value of 7.5 percent, enter the following formula in the worksheet:

@IRR(.075,B3..G3)

@NPV

The Net Present Value Function

This function evaluates a series of future values by adjusting them to determine their present value equivalents. It calculates the net present value of a series of future cash flows according to the discount rate specified.

SYNTAX

@NPV(*int,range*)

where *int* is the discount rate, and *range* is the range of values or cells containing values that represent the future cash flows. The period of the discount rate (usually annual) must agree with that of the cash flows. Also, to obtain the correct net present value, make sure that the period intervals between the cash flows are constant.

EXAMPLE

To calculate the net present value for a series of monthly cash flows entered in the range B10..F10 for an annual periodic interest rate of 15 percent, enter the following formula in the worksheet:

@NPV(.15/12,B10..F10)

Note that the 15 percent annual interest rate is divided by 12 because the cash flows are monthly.

@PMT

The Payment Function

This function calculates the payment required to amortize a loan amount, given the beginning amount of the principal, the interest rate, and the number of payment periods.

SYNTAX

@PMT(*prin,int,term*)

where *prin* is the amount of the loan (that is, the beginning principal), *int* is the periodic interest rate, and *term* is the number of payment periods of the loan.

USAGE

The @PMT function provides an extremely easy method for determining the loan payment required to borrow specific amounts at a fixed rate of interest. When you use this function, the period of the interest rate must agree with that of the term. To convert an annual interest rate to its monthly equivalent, divide it by 12. To convert the term expressed in years into the number of monthly payments, multiply it by 12.

EXAMPLES

To calculate the monthly loan payment required when borrowing $100,000.00 for a term of 15 years at an annual interest rate of 9.875 percent, enter the following formula in the worksheet:

@PMT(100000,0.09875/12,15*12)

Lotus 1-2-3 will calculate that a monthly payment of $1,066.97 is required.

@PV

The Present Value Function

This function calculates the present value of an annuity, given the payment per period and the discount rate over the period of payments specified as the term.

SYNTAX

@PV(*pmt,int,term*)

where *pmt* is the payment per period, *int* is the discount rate, and *term* is the number of payment periods.

USAGE

The @PV function is used much like @NPV to determine the current value of future payments. However, unlike @NPV, it requires the cash flows (specified as the *pmt* argument) to be equal—thus the difference in the arguments required by the function. When you use this function, the period of the interest rate must agree with that of the term. Also, remember that this function assumes that payments are made at the end of each period in the term specified.

EXAMPLE

To calculate the present value of an annuity where the payment is $218.46, the annual interest rate is 9.75 percent, and the term is 36 months, enter the following formula in the worksheet:

@PV(218.46,.0975/12,36)

Lotus 1-2-3 returns a present value of $6,795.00. Note that the annual interest rate is divided by 12 because the term is expressed in months.

@RATE

The Compound Growth Rate Function

The @RATE function calculates the compound growth rate for an initial investment, given its present and future values. It is used to determine the periodic interest rate at which a present value investment will grow into a future value.

SYNTAX

@RATE(*fv,pv,term*)

where *fv* is the future value of an initial investment, *pv* is its present value, and *term* is the number of compounding periods. Compounding periods are assumed to occur at regular intervals throughout the term. If *term* is expressed in years and you need to determine @RATE for a monthly compounded rate, multiply *term* by 12.

EXAMPLE

To calculate the periodic interest rate required to make an investment of $575.00 grow into $1,500.00 in 12 years, enter the following formula in the worksheet:

@RATE(1500,575,12)

Lotus 1-2-3 returns an interest rate of close to 8.32 percent.

@SLN

The Straight-Line Function

The @SLN function calculates the depreciation of an asset by using the straight-line method.

SYNTAX

@SLN(*cost,salvage,life*)

where *cost* is the original cost of the asset, *salvage* is the salvage or residual value, and *life* is the asset's useful life. This method is useful for calculating depreciation of a fixed asset when one of the accelerated methods is not required. It assumes that the amount depreciated is constant during each period of the useful life. Under this method, the depreciable base (the original cost minus the salvage value) is depreciated to zero.

EXAMPLE

To calculate the amount of depreciation using the straight-line method for an item with an original cost of $10,000.00, a salvage value of $500.00, and a life of five years, enter the following formula:

@SLN(10000,500,5)

Lotus 1-2-3 returns $1,900.00 as the amount of depreciation for the five years.

@SYD

The Sum-of-the-Year's-Digits Function

The @SYD function calculates the depreciation of an asset using the sum-of-the-years'-digits method for determining accelerated depreciation. This method determines accelerated depreciation in which the digits of the period of the useful life are summed and this total is used to fix the depreciation percent for each period. Under this method, the depreciable base (the original cost minus the salvage value) is depreciated to zero.

SYNTAX

@SYD(*cost,salvage,life,period*)

where *cost* is the original cost of the asset, *salvage* is the salvage or residual value, *life* is the useful life of the asset, and *period* is the year in which the depreciation is being calculated.

EXAMPLE

To calculate the depreciation in the first year using the sum-of-the-years'-digits method for an item with an original cost of $10,000.00, a salvage value of $500.00, and a life of five years, enter the following formula:

@SYD(10000,500,5,1)

Lotus 1-2-3 returns $3,166.67 as the amount of depreciation for the first year.

@TERM

The Term Function

The @TERM function calculates the number of periods (that is, the term) required to realize a particular future value from an investment in which equal payments are made at the end of each period at a fixed periodic interest rate.

SYNTAX

@TERM(*pmt,int,fv***)**

where *pmt* is the payment per period, *int* is the periodic interest rate, and *fv* is the future value.

USAGE

This function is useful whenever you need to determine the term required to reach a specific future value of an investment when a series of deposits are made over the term.

When you use this function, the period of the interest rate must agree with that of the term. The @TERM function assumes that payments are made at the end of each period. If you wish to determine the number of periods in which payments are made at the beginning of each period, use the following formula:

@TERM(*pmt,int,fv***/(1 +** *int***))**

where *pmt* is the payment per period, *int* is the periodic interest rate, and *fv* is the future value of the investment.

EXAMPLE

To calculate the term required to realize a future value of $5,000.00 at 7 percent interest when depositing $200.00 a month, enter the following formula in the worksheet:

@TERM(200,.07/12,5000)

Lotus 1-2-3 returns a term of 23.4 months. Note that the annual interest was divided by 12 because the term was to be expressed in months.

13

Date and Time Functions

The Lotus 1-2-3 date functions include @DATE, @DAY, @MONTH, @YEAR, @NOW, and @DATEVALUE. All date functions work with these date serial numbers, which assign a number to each date between January 1, 1900 (0) and December 31, 2099 (73050).

The time functions include @HOUR, @MINUTE, @SECOND, @TIME, and @TIMEVALUE. In addition to these specific time functions, the @NOW function can return the current time when it is used with one of the time display formats.

@DATE

The Date Function

This function enters a specific date, either alone or as part of a formula, into a cell of the spreadsheet.

SYNTAX

@DATE(*yr,month,day*)

where *yr* is the last two digits of the year if the date is in the twentieth century or a number from 100 to 199 for dates between 2000 and 2099. *Month* is the number of the month; and *day* is the number of the day of the month.

USAGE

Unlike the @NOW or @TODAY functions, @DATE enters a date that is static and does not change when the worksheet is recalculated. To format the serial number returned by this function to one of the program's date display formats, use the /Range Format Date command followed by the number of the display format you wish to use (see /Range Format Date for a description of the date display formats).

EXAMPLES

To enter the date February 15, 1988 into cell A15 of your worksheet, move the cell pointer to A15, enter

@DATE(88,2,15)

and press Return.

To format the resulting serial number to the Lotus standard long form, type **/RFD1** and press Return. Cell A15 then displays the date as 15-FEB-88.

@DATEVALUE

The Date Value Function

This function returns the correct date serial number for a date entered as a string (a label entry).

SYNTAX

@DATEVALUE(*date string*)

where *date string* is a date entered as a label that conforms to one of Lotus 1-2-3's date formats. If it does not, this function will return an ERR value in the cell where it is entered. You will also receive an ERR value if the month exceeds 12, the number of days exceeds the normal number of days contained in the given month, or the year exceeds 199 (that is, is not between 1900 and 2099).

The *date string* argument can consist of a cell reference to a cell that contains the date string, or it can be the date string itself enclosed in a pair of quotation marks.

USAGE

The @DATEVALUE function is most useful when the dates in a spreadsheet have been imported from another application in which they had to be entered as date strings, usually in the long international format of MM/DD/YY.

After converting date strings to serial numbers with this function, you then format the serial number calculated by this function to one of the Lotus 1-2-3 date display formats by using the /Range Format Date command.

EXAMPLE

If cell B60 of your worksheet contains the label '10/03/88, you can convert it to a Lotus date serial number in cell C60 by entering

@DATEVALUE(B60)

and pressing Return. To replace the date string with the date serial number, simply convert the formula into its value (by pressing F2, F9, and Return), format it to a Lotus date format, and move it from cell C60 to B60.

NOTES

Certain date strings cannot be converted; they return ERR values in the spreadsheet. This is because these strings do not conform to Lotus 1-2-3 date display formats.

However, if a date string had been entered as 88-10-03 in a cell, it could be successfully converted with @DATEVALUE if the long international display format had been changed with the /Worksheet Global Default Other International Date D command. This is the only display format that allows hyphens between date numbers, though the pattern it requires is always YY-MM-DD.

When only the month and year are specified in the date string, as in 'Oct-88, the @DATEVALUE function returns the serial number equivalent to the first day of the month.

Entering the date string in the format in which the month is completely spelled out followed by the day, a comma, and the four digits of the year—as in October 10, 1988—cannot be accommodated with the @DATEVALUE function.

@DAY

The Day Function

This function returns the number of the day represented by the digits of the date serial number given as the argument.

SYNTAX

@DAY(*date number*)

where *date number* is a serial number between 1 (which returns 1 for January 1, 1900) and 73050 (which returns 31 for December 31, 2099). The *date number* argument can consist of a manual entry, a date function that calculates the number, or a cell reference that contains the date number, which has been either entered manually or calculated by the date functions @NOW or @DATE.

EXAMPLES

To find the day of the month represented by the serial number calculated by entering @DATE(86,11,15) in cell A1, enter the following in the cell where you want the day to appear:

@DAY(A1)

Lotus 1-2-3 returns the value 15.

To return only the day portion of @DATE(86,11,15), which has not yet been entered into another cell of the worksheet, enter the following in the cell where you want the day to appear:

@DAY(@DATE(86,11,15))

Lotus 1-2-3 returns the value 15.

@HOUR

The Hour Function

This function returns the number of the hour between 0 (for 12:00 AM or midnight) and 23 (for 11:00 PM) represented in the time serial number entered as the argument.

SYNTAX

@HOUR(*time number*)

where *time number* is a value between 0.000, which returns the hour 0 for midnight, and 0.9999, which returns the hour of 11:00 PM. If the argument is a mixed number, only the decimal part of the value is used to determine the hour. If the argument is an integer, the function uses 0.000 as the time value and returns the hour of midnight (0).

The *time number* argument can be another time function (such as @NOW, @TIME, or @TIMEVALUE), a fractional serial number, or a calculation that results in such a number.

USAGE

This function is often used to return only the hour portion of a time value entered with the @TIME or @NOW functions. It can also be used to return the hour of the day from a decimal value representing the fractional serial number that is entered manually or calculated by a formula that does not use the @TIME function.

EXAMPLES

To determine the hour of the day when you enter the decimal equivalent of the time of day, enter the formula in the following way:

@HOUR(0.8567)

It returns a value of 20 or 8:00 PM.

To determine the hour of the day when entering a calculation as the argument, enter the formula like this:

@HOUR(6.5/12.75)

It returns a value of 12 or 12:00 PM.

You can also combine the @HOUR function with the @TIME or @NOW function. For example, if you enter the function @TIME(7,45,15) in cell A1 and then enter the formula

@HOUR(A1)

Lotus 1-2-3 returns the value 7 in the cell where this function is entered.

@MINUTE

The Minute Function

This function returns the number of the minute between 0 and 59 represented in the time serial number entered as the argument.

SYNTAX

@MINUTE(*time number*)

where *time number* is a value between 0.000 and 0.9999. If the argument is a mixed number, only the decimal part of the value is used to determine the minute. If the argument is an integer, the function uses 0.000 as the time value and returns the minute 0.

The time number argument can be another time function, such as @NOW, @TIME, or @TIMEVALUE; a fractional serial number; or a calculation that results in such a number.

USAGE

This function is useful whenever you need to work with only the minute portion of the time either in data entry in the spreadsheet or when using formulas to calculate new time values. Like the @HOUR function, @MINUTE can be used with the time functions @NOW, @TIME, and @TIMEVALUE to return only the number of minutes from their calculated time numbers.

EXAMPLES

To determine the minute when you enter the decimal equivalent of the time of day, enter the formula as follows:

@MINUTE(0.8567)

It returns a value of 33 minutes.

To determine the minute of the hour when entering a calculation as the argument, enter the formula like this:

@MINUTE(6.5/12.75)

It returns a value of 14 minutes.

You can also combine the @MINUTE function with the @TIME or @NOW function. For example, you can enter the function @TIME(7,45,15) in cell A1 and then enter the formula

@MINUTE(A1)

Lotus 1-2-3 returns the value 45 in the cell where this function is entered.

@MONTH

The Month Function

This function returns the number of the month represented by the digits of the date serial number given as the argument.

SYNTAX

@MONTH(*date number*)

where *date number* is a serial number between 0 (which returns 1 for January) and 73050 (which returns 12 for December). It can consist of a manual entry, a date function that calculates the number, or a cell reference containing the date number that has been either entered manually or calculated by the date functions @NOW or @DATE. Most of the time, the date number is supplied by using another of the date functions to calculate it.

EXAMPLES

To find the month represented by the serial number calculated by entering @DATE(86,11,15) in cell A1, enter the following in the cell where you want the month to appear:

@MONTH(A1)

Lotus 1-2-3 returns the value 11.

To return only the month portion of @DATE(86,11,15), which has not yet been entered into another cell of the worksheet, enter the following in the cell where you want the month to appear:

@MONTH(@DATE(86,11,15))

Lotus 1-2-3 returns the value 11.

@NOW

The Current Date and Time Function

This function enters into a cell the current date and time supplied by the system as a serial number.

SYNTAX

@NOW

This function takes no arguments.

USAGE

The @NOW function takes the current date and time as entered in response to the DOS DATE and TIME commands and converts them into a serial number. The @NOW function calculates a serial number that includes a decimal value representing the time of day as well as digits representing the date. You can then format this serial number into one of five date formats or four time formats (see /Range Format Date for a description of the date formats).

You can also use this function in formulas to perform date or time arithmetic that depends on the current date. It can be referenced by other Lotus 1-2-3 date and time functions—@YEAR, @MONTH, @DAY, @HOUR, @MINUTE, and @SECOND—to return just the part of the current date or time controlled by the function.

When you enter the date and time into a cell by using the @NOW function, they are automatically updated whenever the worksheet is recalculated. This means that the date and time will be made current as soon as the worksheet is recalculated.

EXAMPLES

To enter the current date into cell A1 in a worksheet, move the cell pointer to this cell, type

@NOW

and press Return.

To format the serial number to the Lotus standard long form (DD-MMM-YY), type **/RFD1** and press Return. Then widen the cell to 10 characters (**/WCS10**), if necessary.

@SECOND

The Second Function

This function returns the number of seconds between 0 and 59 represented in the time serial number entered as the argument. It is useful whenever you need to work with only the seconds portion of the time either in data entry in the spreadsheet or when using formulas to calculate new time values.

SYNTAX

@SECOND(*time number*)

where *time number* is a value between 0.000 and 0.9999. If the argument is a mixed number, only the decimal part of the value is used to determine the seconds. If the argument is an integer, the function uses 0.000 as the time value and returns a seconds value of 0. The time number argument can be another time function, such as @NOW, @TIME, or @TIMEVALUE; a fractional serial number; or a calculation that results in such a number.

EXAMPLES

To determine the second when you enter the decimal equivalent of the time of day, enter the formula as follows:

@SECOND(0.8567)

It returns a value of 39 seconds.

To determine the number of seconds when entering a calculation as the argument, enter the formula like this:

@SECOND(6.5/12.75)

It returns a value of 7 seconds.

@TIME

The Time Function

This function returns the decimal equivalent of the time of day according to the values entered as arguments for the function.

SYNTAX

@TIME(*hr,min,sec*)

where *hr* is the number of the hour between 0 (for midnight) and 23 (for 11:00 PM), *min* is the number of minutes between 0 and 59, and *sec* is the number of seconds between 0 and 59. If any of these argument values are larger, the function will return an ERR value. The arguments can be literal values or references to cells that contain such literal or calculated values, entered either by cell address or range name.

USAGE

When you use the @TIME function, Lotus 1-2-3 returns the decimal equivalent of the time of day in the cell. You can then format the display by using the /Range Format Date Time command and choosing one of the time display formats (see /Range Format Date for a description of time display formats).

EXAMPLE

To enter the time 3:45 PM into cell D14 of your worksheet, move the cell pointer to this cell, enter

@TIME(15,45,0)

and press Return. To format the resulting decimal value to one of Lotus 1-2-3's time formats, type **/RFDT**, select the desired format number, and press Return again.

@TIMEVALUE

The Time Value Function

This function returns the correct time serial number for the time entered as a string (a label entry).

SYNTAX

@TIMEVALUE(*time string*)

where *time string* is a time entered as a label that conforms to one of Lotus 1-2-3's time formats. If it does not, this function will return an ERR value in the cell where it is entered. You will also receive an ERR value if the hour exceeds 23 or if the minutes or seconds exceed 59.

The *time string* argument can consist of a cell reference to a cell that contains the time string, or it can be the time string itself enclosed in a pair of quotation marks.

The program assumes that hours between 1 and 11 are AM times unless the time string contains the PM designation.

USAGE

The @TIMEVALUE function is most useful when the times in a spreadsheet have been imported from another application in which they had to be entered as time strings, usually in the format HH:MM:SS AM/PM. You can then format the fractional serial number calculated by this function to one of the Lotus 1-2-3 time display formats by using the /Range Format Date Time command and choosing the number of the format you wish to use.

EXAMPLES

If cell F10 of your worksheet contains the label '10:30 PM, you can convert it to a decimal number in cell G10 by moving the cell pointer to this cell, entering

@TIMEVALUE(F10)

and pressing Return. To replace the time string with the calculated time decimal number, convert the formula into its value (by pressing F2, F9, and Return), format it to a Lotus time format, and then move it from cell G10 to F10.

@YEAR

The Year Function

This function returns the number of the year represented by the digits of the date serial number given as the argument.

SYNTAX

@YEAR(*date number*)

where *date number* is a serial number between 0 (which returns 0 for 1900) and 73050 (which returns 199 for 2099). Most of the time, the date number is supplied by using another of the date functions to calculate it, although it can be entered manually.

USAGE

The date number used as the argument of the @YEAR function can consist of a manual entry, a date function that calculates the number, or a cell reference that contains the date number, which has been either manually entered or calculated by the date function @NOW or @DATE.

EXAMPLES

To find the year represented by the serial number calculated by entering @DATE(86,11,15) in cell A1, enter the following in the cell where you want the year to appear:

@YEAR(A1)

Lotus 1-2-3 returns the value 86.

To return only the year portion of @DATE(86,11,15), which has not yet been entered into another cell of the worksheet, enter the following in the cell where you want the year to appear:

@YEAR(@DATE(86,11,15))

Lotus 1-2-3 returns the value 86.

You can also return the digits of the current year in a cell by using @NOW (or @TODAY) as the argument of the @YEAR function. Enter it as follows:

@YEAR(@NOW)

14

Logical Functions

The logical functions include @IF, @ISAAF, @ISAPP, @ISNA, @ISERR, @ISNUMBER, @ISSTRING, @TRUE, and @FALSE. Logical functions assign the value 1 as the true value and 0 as the false value. They all evaluate the contents of a specific cell in the worksheet and return either 0 or 1, depending on whether a particular condition exists.

@FALSE

The False Function

The @FALSE function returns the logical value 0.

SYNTAX

@FALSE

This function takes no arguments.

USAGE

When used alone, the @FALSE function always returns the value 0 in the cell where it is entered. The @FALSE function is often combined with the @IF function so that its calculation of a zero value is used only when the condition stated does not exist in the spreadsheet. This makes it useful in situations where you need to validate and document whether a particular condition exists in another part of the worksheet.

In such an application, the @FALSE function is used as the *y* argument of the @IF condition (the @TRUE function is most often the *x* argument or true value). This allows you to determine quickly which cells fail the condition.

EXAMPLES

The following example illustrates the use of the @FALSE function as an argument of an @IF function to validate the failure of a particular condition in the spreadsheet:

```
@IF(@AVG(C5..C8)<75000,@TRUE,@FALSE)
```

Zero (0) is returned in the cell where this formula is entered if the average of the figures in the range of cells indicated as the argument of the @AVG function is above 75,000.

@IF

The If Function

The @IF function evaluates the condition that makes up its first argument. If the condition is true, it returns the value entered as the second argument (the *x* value). If the condition is false, it returns the value given as the third argument (the *y* value).

SYNTAX

@IF(*cond,x,y*)

where *cond* is a conditional statement in the form of an equation or inequality, *x* is the value returned if the conditional statement is found to be true, and *y* is the value returned if the conditional statement is found to be false.

The conditional statement can contain a literal or calculated value, or a cell reference to such values in the logical formula. The logical formula is separated by one or more of the logical or Boolean operators and can also contain mathematical operators if a calculation is called for within the statement to be evaluated.

The *x* and *y* arguments can contain literal values or cell references to literal values, calculations of some sort, or other Lotus 1-2-3 functions, including more @IF functions. The arguments can also contain string values, as long as they are enclosed in a pair of quotation marks.

USAGE

The @IF function provides a powerful means not only for evaluating whether a particular condition exists in the spreadsheet but also for having the program take a particular action, depending on the outcome of the evaluation.

The @IF function allows you to combine the other logical functions within it, enabling you to incorporate the particular type of testing each function is designed to do in the condition you develop.

The @IF function also allows you to build complex conditions using the Boolean operators AND, OR, and NOT in addition to the full group of logical operators. Other @IF functions can also be nested within the basic @IF function, providing you with multiple branches off the original condition to cover all possible conditions that can arise and must be accounted for.

EXAMPLES

At the most basic level, the @IF function can be used to choose between two alternate calculations that should take place, depending on the value of a particular cell:

```
@IF(K12<30000,K12*1.33,K12*1.5)
```

In this formula, the value in K12 is increased by 1.33 only when its value is below $30,000.00; otherwise, its value is increased 1.5 times.

Many times, the possible alternatives are not limited to two, as in the preceding example. In such situations, you can expand the basic @IF function to accommodate all of the possibilities by combining @IF conditions:

```
@IF(R2>=50000,@IF(R2<=75000,R2*.04,R2*.10),R2*.02)
```

In this example, you are testing for three possibilities: first, that the value in R2 will be below $50,000.00; second, that it will be greater than or equal to $50,000.00 but still be equal to or below $75,000.00; or, third, that it will be above $75,000.00.

@ISAAF

2.2

The Is Add-In @Function Function

The @ISAAF function returns the logical value 1 (true) if its argument is the name of a defined add-in @function. It returns the logical value 0 (false) if the cell contains any other string.

SYNTAX

@ISAAF(name)

where *name* is a string, a string formula, or a single cell reference that contains a label.

EXAMPLES

@ISAAF can be used to test whether an @function is an add-in @function. Assume that the following function is placed in cell E45:

@ISAAF("SUM")

If @SUM is an add-in @function, instead of the built-in @SUM function, cell E45 will contain 1. If @SUM is not defined as an add-in @function, or it has been defined but not attached (see /Add-In), E45 will contain 0.

@ISAFF can also be used in a conditional statement. If you do not want to sum a set of numbers unless the @SUM add-in is present, you can use a statement like

@IF(@ISAAF("SUM",@SUM(C13..C20),0))

In this example, the range C13..C20 is summed only if @SUM is an add-in @function. If not, this cell will contain 0.

NOTE

Do not include the @ symbol in the argument you pass to @ISAAF.

SEE ALSO

/Add-In

@ISAPP

2.2

The Is Add-In Program Function

The @ISAPP function returns the logical value 1 (true) if its argument is the name of a defined add-in program. It returns the logical value 0 (false) if the cell contains any other string.

SYNTAX

@ISAPP*(name)*

where name is a string, a string formula, or a single cell reference that contains a label.

EXAMPLES

The @ISAPP function can be used to test whether an Add-In program is attached. Assume that the following function is placed in cell E45:

@ISAPP("ALLWAYS")

If ALLWAYS is an add-in program, cell E45 will contain 1. If Allways is not defined as an add-in, or if it has been defined but not attached, E45 will contain 0.

@ISAPP can also be used in a conditional statement. If you want a cell to contain a number only if ALLWAYS is present, you can use a statement like

@IF(@ISAPP("ALLWAYS",45,0))

In this example, the cell contains 45 only if Allways has been attached. If not, this cell will contain 0.

NOTE

Do not include the .ADN extension in the argument you pass to @ISAPP.

SEE ALSO

/Add-In

@ISERR

The Is ERR Function

The @ISERR function evaluates the *x* value given as its argument and returns the logical value 1 (true) when the value is ERR. It returns the logical value 0 (false) if the cell contains any other numeric value or a string.

SYNTAX

@ISERR(*x*)

where *x* is a single cell reference that contains a literal value or one calculated by formula.

EXAMPLES

The @ISERR function can be used alone to check for the existence of an ERR value in a particular cell. Assume in the following example that the @ISERR function is entered into cell AB50 in the spreadsheet:

@ISERR(F50)

If cell F50 contains an ERR value, cell AB50 will contain 1 to indicate this. If cell F50 contains any other kind of value or a label, AB50 will contain 0, indicating that the ERR value is not present there.

To prevent the proliferation of ERR values in a spreadsheet with formulas that depend on a specific value, the @ISERR function is often combined with an @IF function, as follows:

@IF(@ISERR(X10),0,@IF(X10<15000,X10*1.5,X10))

In this example, the value 0 is returned in the cell where this formula is entered if the presence of an ERR value is detected in cell X10. Only if X10 does not contain an ERR value will Lotus 1-2-3 go ahead and evaluate the second @IF condition, and, depending on the value it contains, either multiply that value by 1.5 or use it as is.

NOTES

Using zero as the *x* argument of an @IF condition containing an @ISERR function works only when the cell reference supplied as the argument of the @ISERR function is not used as a denominator in division in any of the dependent formulas (division by zero is one of the major causes of ERR values in spreadsheets).

@ISNA

The Is NA Function

The @ISNA function evaluates the *x* value given as its argument and returns the logical value 1 (true) when the value is NA. It returns the logical value 0 (false) if the cell contains any other numeric value or a string.

SYNTAX

@ISNA(*x*)

where *x* is a single cell reference that contains a label, value, or formula.

EXAMPLES

The @ISNA function can be used alone to test for the presence of the NA value in a specific cell. Assume that you enter the following formula in cell B40:

@ISNA(B5)

The result is 1 in B40 if B5 contains NA, and 0 if B5 contains any other value or a label. Cell B5 would contain an NA value if the @NA function had been entered into it or if it were dependent on some other formula in which the @NA function was entered.

To prevent the proliferation of NA values into cells in other parts of the spreadsheet (assuming that they contain formulas dependent on the value calculated in B40), you could combine this formula with an @IF function:

@IF(@ISNA(B5),0,B11/B5)

In this example, zero is returned in B40 if B5 contains the NA value. Only when B5 does not contain NA does the program attempt to divide the value in B11 by B5. This prevents the ERR value being calculated in B40, which would result from attempting to divide a numeric value in B11 by an NA value in B5.

@ISNUMBER

The Is Number Function

The @ISNUMBER function evaluates the *x* value given as its argument and returns the logical value 1 (true) when *x* is found to contain any type of numerical value (including ERR and NA values) and when it is blank. It returns the logical value 0 (false) if the cell contains a string.

SYNTAX

@ISNUMBER(*x*)

where *x* is a single cell reference that contains a literal value or one calculated by formula.

USAGE

This function is most useful when you need to ascertain that a particular cell in the spreadsheet contains a numeric value rather than a string value, which would result in an ERR value if it were used in another dependent formula calculation.

Although you can use the @ISNUMBER function by itself to test whether a specific cell contains a value or string, it is most often used with the @IF function so that you can control what happens when the test fails (indicating that the cell does contain some sort of label).

EXAMPLES

To make a simple test for the presence of a value in a cell, enter the @ISNUMBER function as follows:

@ISNUMBER(D25)

This formula returns 1 if D25 contains a value or is blank and 0 if it contains some sort of label (string).

More often, you will want to combine the @ISNUMBER function with the @IF function as part of the stated condition:

@IF(@ISNUMBER(D25),D25*1.5,"LABEL")

The condition checks for the presence of a value in cell D25 before multiplying it by 1.5. If D25 does not contain a value, the message *LABEL* appears instead to alert you that D25 must be edited.

@ISSTRING

The Is String Function

The @ISSTRING function evaluates the *x* value given as its argument and returns the logical value 1 (true) when *x* is found to contain a string value (label). It returns the logical value 0 (false) when the cell contains any kind of numerical value or is blank.

SYNTAX

@ISSTRING(*x*)

where *x* is a single cell reference that contains a literal value or one calculated by a formula.

USAGE

This function is the logical counterpart of the @ISNUMBER function. It is used when you need to ascertain that a particular cell in the spreadsheet contains a label rather than a value.

Although you can use the @ISSTRING function by itself to test whether a specific cell contains a string or value, it is most often used with the @IF function, so that you can control what happens when the test fails (indicating that the cell does contain some sort of value).

EXAMPLES

To make a simple test for the presence of a label in a cell, enter the @ISSTRING function as follows:

@ISSTRING(C10)

This formula returns 1 if C10 contains a string value (that is, was entered as a label); otherwise, it returns 0.

More often, you will want to combine the @ISSTRING function with the @IF function as part of a stated condition:

@IF(@ISSTRING(C10)#AND#@ISSTRING(D10), C10&" "&D10,"VALUE")

This condition checks for the presence of labels in cells C10 and D10 before attempting to combine their contents in the cell where this formula is entered. If either C10 or D10 does not contain a string, the message *VALUE* appears instead to alert you that one of these cells must be edited before the concatenation can take place.

@TRUE

The True Function

The @TRUE function returns the logical value 1.

SYNTAX

@TRUE

This function takes no arguments.

USAGE

When used alone, the @TRUE function returns the value 1 in the cell where the function is entered. When combined with the @IF function (as the x argument), it offers a convenient method for validating and documenting the existence of the condition stated as the conditional argument. If the condition exists, the value 1 is entered into the cell where the @IF function is used.

Usually in such cases, the @FALSE function is used as the y argument so that the logical value 1 for true is counterbalanced by the logical value 0 for false. This provides a convenient method for visually checking the existence of a condition elsewhere in the spreadsheet that may not be obvious when scanning the data.

EXAMPLES

The example below illustrates the use of the @TRUE function as an argument of an @IF function to validate the existence of a particular condition in the spreadsheet:

@IF(@NOW – A4 > = 45,@TRUE,@FALSE)

Cell A4 holds the invoice date. In this condition, the @IF function tests whether the invoice has aged 45 or more days by subtracting the invoice date from the current date. If it has, the function places 1 in the cell where this function is entered.

15

Database Statistical Functions

The database statistical functions all require the same three types of arguments: an input range, an offset number, and a criteria range. Their use is often combined to obtain meaningful statistics describing the data contained in the database. These functions include @DAVG, @DCOUNT, @DMAX, @DMIN, @DSTD, @DSUM, and @DVAR.

@DAVG

The Data Average Function

This function calculates the average or mean of the values in a specific column of the data table given as the offset argument, according to the criteria set up in the criteria range.

SYNTAX

@DAVG(*input,offset,criteria*)

where *input* is the input range containing both a single row of unique column designations (field names) and all of the rows of data in the table; *offset* is the number of the column to be averaged, starting with 0 as the leftmost column; and *criteria* is the criteria range, which includes duplicates of the column designations with the criteria entered in the cells directly beneath each.

The *input* and *criteria* arguments can be designated by the cell addresses of the range or by range name if one has been previously assigned. The *offset* argument is usually entered as a literal value, although it can also be a cell reference to such a value. If no criterion is entered beneath the column designator in the criteria range, all of the data in the column specified by the offset argument is used in determining the average.

USAGE

Because the @DAVG function calculates the average by calculating the sum and dividing it by the count, it is possible to obtain skewed results if the criteria range allows zero values and the column contains labels (in which case @DAVG returns ERR). When calculating the sum, labels (which carry zero values) do not affect the total; however, as nonblank cells they do increase the count. Blank cells within a column do not affect the @DAVG function.

EXAMPLES

To find the average salary below $50,000 in a salary field of a Lotus 1-2-3 database, enter the @DAVG formula

@DAVG(A4..H400,3,J4..J5)

where the database occupies the cell range A4..H400; the salary field is the fourth field in column D; and the criteria range is J4..J5 and contains the formula +D4<50000.

@DCOUNT

The Data Count Function

This function returns the number of nonblank cells in a specific column of the data table given as the offset argument, according to the criteria set up in the criteria range.

SYNTAX

@DCOUNT(*input,offset,criteria*)

where *input* is the input range containing both a single row of unique column designations (field names) and all of the rows of data in the table; *offset* is the number of the column to be counted, starting with 0 as the leftmost column; and *criteria* is the criteria range, which includes duplicates of the column designations with the criteria entered in the cells directly beneath each.

The input and criteria arguments can be designated by the cell addresses of the range or by range name if one has been previously assigned. The offset argument is usually entered as a literal value, although it can also be a cell reference to such a value.

USAGE

The @DCOUNT function obtains the number of nonblank cells in a range of entries in a particular column of the database. If no criteria are entered beneath the column designator in the criteria range, all of the data in the column specified by the offset argument is used in determining the count.

EXAMPLES

To find the number of entries where the salary is below $50,000 in a salary field of a Lotus 1-2-3 database, enter the @DCOUNT formula

@DCOUNT(A4..H400,3,J4..J5)

where the database occupies the cell range A4..H400; the salary field is the fourth field in column D; and the criteria range is J4..J5 and contains the formula +D4<50000.

@DMAX

The Data Maximum Function

The @DMAX function returns the maximum value in a specific column of the data table given as the offset argument, according to the criteria set up in the criteria range.

SYNTAX

@DMAX(*input,offset,criteria*)

where *input* is the input range containing both a single row of unique column designations (field names) and all of the rows of data in the table; *offset* is the number of the column to be evaluated, starting with 0 as the leftmost column; and *criteria* is the criteria range, which includes duplicates of the column designations with the criteria entered in the cells directly beneath each.

The input and criteria arguments can be designated by the cell addresses of the range or by range name, if one has been previously assigned. The offset argument is usually entered as a literal value, although it can also be a cell reference to such a value.

USAGE

The @DMAX function obtains the highest value in a range of values in a particular column of a database. If no criteria are entered beneath the column designator in the criteria range, all of the data in the column specified by the offset argument is evaluated when determining the maximum value.

When this function is used in a column of the database that contains date values (entered with the @DATE function), it returns the most recent date as the maximum value.

EXAMPLES

To find the highest salary below $50,000 in a salary field of a Lotus 1-2-3 database, enter the @DMAX formula

@DMAX(A4..H400,3,J4..J5)

where the database occupies the cell range A4..H400; the salary field is the fourth field in column D; and the criteria range is J4..J5 and contains the formula +D4<50000.

@DMIN

The Data Minimum Function

This function returns the minimum value in a specific column of the database given as the offset argument, according to the criteria set up in the criteria range.

SYNTAX

@DMIN(*input,offset,criteria*)

where *input* is the input range containing both a single row of unique column designations (field names) and all of the rows of data in the table; *offset* is the number of the column to be evaluated, starting with 0 as the leftmost column; and *criteria* is the criteria range, which includes duplicates of the column designations with the criteria entered in the cells directly beneath each.

The input and criteria arguments can be designated by the cell addresses of the range or by range name if one has been previously assigned. The offset argument is usually entered as a literal value, although it can also be a cell reference to such a value.

USAGE

The @DMIN function is used to obtain the lowest value in a range of values in a particular column of database. If no criteria are entered beneath the column designator in the criteria range, all of the data in the column specified by the offset argument is evaluated when determining the minimum value.

When this function is used in a column of the database that contains date values (entered with the @DATE function), it returns the oldest date as the minimum value, because dates are converted to serial numbers and older dates have smaller serial numbers.

EXAMPLES

To find the lowest salary below $50,000 in a salary field of a Lotus 1-2-3 database, enter the @DMIN formula

@DMIN(A4..H400,3,J4..J5)

where the database occupies the cell range A4..H400; the salary field is the fourth field in column D; and the criteria range is J4..J5 and contains the formula +D4<50000.

@DSTD

The Data Standard Deviation Function

This function returns the standard deviation (*S*) of the values in a specific column of the database given as the offset argument, according to the criteria set up in the criteria range.

SYNTAX

@DSTD(*input,offset,criteria*)

where *input* is the input range containing both a single row of unique column designations (field names) and all of the rows of data in the table; *offset* is the number of the column to be evaluated, starting with 0 as the leftmost column; and *criteria* is the criteria range, which includes duplicates of the column designations with the criteria entered in the cells directly beneath each.

The input and criteria arguments can be designated by the cell addresses of the range or by range name if one has been previously assigned. The offset argument is usually entered as a literal value, although it can also be a cell reference to such a value.

USAGE

The @DSTD function calculates the standard deviation, which is a statistical measurement of the degree to which an individual score in a range of values in a particular column of database varies from its mean score. If no criteria are entered beneath the column designator in the criteria range, all of the data in the column specified by the offset argument is evaluated when determining the standard deviation.

With the @DSTD function, misplaced label entries in the column can skew the result of the mean value and thus that of the standard deviation if the criteria allow zero values in the criteria range.

EXAMPLE

To find the standard deviation of salaries below $50,000 in a salary field of a Lotus 1-2-3 database, enter the @DSTD formula

@DSTD(A4..H400,3,J4..J5)

where the database occupies the cell range A4..H400; the salary field is the fourth field in column D; and the criteria range is J4..J5 and contains the formula +D4<50000.

@DSUM

The Data Sum Function

This function calculates the total of the values in a specific column of the data table given as the offset argument, according to the criteria set up in the criteria range.

SYNTAX

@DSUM(*input,offset,criteria*)

where *input* is the input range containing both a single row of unique column designations (field names) and all of the rows of data in the table; *offset* is the number of the column to be summed, starting with 0 as the leftmost column; and *criteria* is the criteria range, which includes duplicates of the column designations with the criteria entered in the cells directly beneath each.

The input and criteria arguments can be designated by the cell addresses of the range or by range name if one has been previously assigned. The offset argument is usually entered as a literal value, although it can also be a cell reference to such a value.

USAGE

The @DSUM function obtains totals of specific values in a database. If no criteria is entered beneath the column designator in the criteria range, all of the data in the column specified by the offset number is summed.

If you wish to obtain the total for only part of the values in a column of the database, set up a criteria formula that limits the range of values to be included.

EXAMPLE

To find the total of the salaries below $50,000 in a salary field of a Lotus 1-2-3 database, enter the @DSUM formula

@DSUM(A4..H400,3,J4..J5)

where the database occupies the cell range A4..H400; the salary field is the fourth field in column D; and the criteria range is J4..J5 and contains the formula +D4<50000.

@DVAR

The Data Variance Function

This function returns the variance (S^2) of the values in a specific column of the database given as the offset argument, according to the criteria set up in the criteria range.

SYNTAX

@DVAR(*input,offset,criteria*)

where *input* is the input range, containing both a single row of unique column designations (field names) and all of the rows of data in the table; *offset* is the number of the column to be evaluated, starting with 0 as the leftmost column; and *criteria* is the criteria range, which includes duplicates of the column designations with the criteria entered in the cells directly beneath each.

The input and criteria arguments can be designated by the cell addresses of the range or by range name if one has been previously assigned. The offset argument is usually entered as a literal value, although it can also be a cell reference to such a value.

USAGE

The @DVAR function calculates the variance, which is a statistical measurement of the degree to which an individual score in a range of values in a particular column of a database varies from its mean score. This statistic is equal to the square of the standard deviation. If no criteria are entered beneath the column designator in the criteria range, all of the data in the column specified by the offset argument is evaluated when calculating the variance.

When you use the @DVAR function, misplaced label entries in the column can skew the result of the mean value and consequently that of the variance if the criteria allow zero values in the criteria range.

EXAMPLE

To find the variance of the salaries below $50,000 in a salary field of a Lotus 1-2-3 database, enter the @DVAR formula

@DVAR(A4..H400,3,J4..J5)

where the database occupies the cell range A4..H400; the salary field is the fourth field in column D; and the criteria range is J4..J5 and contains the formula +D4<50000.

16

String Functions

The string functions perform a wide variety of tasks on character strings (labels) used in the worksheet. Although the string functions can sometimes be useful when you are developing a spreadsheet or database application manually, they are more often used in macros that process data containing character strings.

@CHAR

The LICS Character Function

The @CHAR function returns the appropriate LICS (Lotus International Character Set) character for the code supplied as its argument.

SYNTAX

@CHAR(*x*)

where *x* is a value between 0 and 255 representing one of the 256 LICS codes. The x argument can be entered as a value or as a cell reference to such a value. If the value is not between 0 and 255, the function will return an ERR value. If the value is below 32, the character will not print on your screen. (Note that 32, the code for a space, is also not a visible character.)

USAGE

The @CHAR function can be used to enter one of the printable LICS characters in the spreadsheet. It must be used instead of the

Compose key (Alt-F1) and compose character sequence when creating a macro to enter such codes, since the {COMPOSE} symbol is not recognized as a macro keyword.

Lotus 1-2-3 returns the LICS character in the cell, and the literal contents of the cell contain the formula. To convert this formula to the LICS character, press the Edit (F2) and Calc (F9) keys to replace it with its literal string or numeric value.

EXAMPLE

To enter the address "119 Av. des Champs-Élysées" in Paris into a database, enter the following formula in the appropriate cell:

+"119 Av. des Champs-"&@CHAR(201)
&"lys"&@CHAR(233)&"es"

@CHAR(201) enters the capital E with the acute accent, and @CHAR(233) enters the lowercase e with the acute accent. You could then copy this formula and edit the street numbers for all addresses on this avenue.

@CLEAN

The Clean String Function

The @CLEAN function removes any nonprintable ASCII characters contained in the string supplied as its argument.

SYNTAX

@CLEAN(*string*)

where *string* is any character string entered between a pair of quotation marks or is a reference to a cell that contains a label entry.

USAGE

The @CLEAN function is required only when you import data that contains (or is suspected of containing) nonprintable ASCII codes generated in another program.

EXAMPLES

To ensure that a particular label imported into cell A2 contains no nonprintable ASCII characters, move the cell pointer to B2 and enter

@CLEAN(A2)

If you had an entire column of such labels, you could then copy the formula in column B down the rows.

@CODE

The ASCII/LICS Code Function

This function returns the ASCII/LICS code of the first character of the string supplied as its argument.

SYNTAX

@CODE(*string*)

where *string* is any character string entered between a pair of quotation marks or is a reference to a cell that contains a label entry.

USAGE

The @CODE function is useful whenever you need to know the ASCII code for a particular printable symbol or letter and do not have access to the LICS or ASCII code chart.

If the cell referenced in the argument of the @CODE function contains more than a single character, only the code of the initial character will be returned. These code numbers are not prefaced by 0, so you will have to add it when using the code in embedded printing commands.

EXAMPLE

To find the ASCII/LICS code for the capital letter A, enter

@CODE("A")

The program returns the value 65 in the cell where this formula was entered. To obtain the ASCII code for the lowercase *a* in the label "after tax" in cell C10, enter

@CODE(C10)

The program returns the value 97, which is the value of the first letter, lowercase *a*, in "after tax".

@EXACT

The Exact String Function

This function compares the two strings supplied as its arguments and returns the logical value 1 for true if they match exactly and the logical value 0 if they are different. The function is case-sensitive.

SYNTAX

@EXACT(*string1,string2*)

where *string1* and *string2* are either character strings entered between a pair of quotation marks, or references to cells that contain the label entries to be compared to one another.

EXAMPLE

To use the @EXACT function to compare the label in cell A5 in the spreadsheet against the string "Closing costs", enter

@EXACT(A5,"Closing costs")

in the cell where you want the result to appear. If, for instance, A5 contains the label Closing Costs, this function returns the value 0, showing that there was no exact match (the capitalization is different).

@FIND

The Find String Function

The @FIND function returns the value of the position of a substring contained in another string. It starts its search for the substring from the position indicated as the *start number* argument.

SYNTAX

@FIND(*search string,string,start number*)

where *search string* is the substring to be located, *string* is the overall string that contains the search string, and *start number* marks the position in the string where the search is to begin.

The *search string* and *string* arguments can be supplied by entering the string enclosed in quotation marks or by cell reference to cells containing these strings. The *start number* can be entered as a value or as a reference to a cell containing such a value. The start number is computed from 0, marking the position of the first character, and is increased by one for every character to the right.

USAGE

This command performs a search for the string given as its first argument in the string supplied as its second argument. The search is for an exact match not only between characters but also between their capitalization. Lotus 1-2-3 begins the search from the position entered as its third argument.

If no match for the substring is located in the string or if the start number specified is greater than the number of positions in the string, the function returns an ERR value. When the function locates its first match for the search string, it returns the position of the first character in that search string.

EXAMPLES

To determine the position of the first occurrence of the string "value" in the label "Market value/Book value ratio" entered in cell A23, enter the formula

@FIND("value",A23,0)

It calculates 7 as the position of the *v* in the first occurrence of the substring "value". If you then want to test this same string in A3 to determine whether it contains another occurrence of "value" and where it is located, enter

@FIND("value",A23,8)

It returns 18 as the position of the *v* in the second occurrence of the word. The start number in this formula was given as 8 because the first formula returned the value of 7. By adding one more to this number, you ensure that the program will bypass the first occurrence and evaluate only any subsequent appearances of the search string.

@LEFT

The Left String Function

The @LEFT function extracts the number of characters designated as its *n* argument from the beginning of the string specified as its first argument.

SYNTAX

@LEFT(*string,n*)

where *string* is any character string entered between a pair of quotation marks or is a reference to a cell that contains a label entry, and *n* is the number of characters to be extracted from the beginning of the string.

USAGE

When you use the @LEFT function, the program will copy the number of characters starting from the beginning of the string into the cell, and they will be left-justified in the cell, like any label. However, the literal contents of the cell will be the formula @LEFT(*string,n*)

To convert this formula to a label entry, press the Edit key (F2) followed by the Calc key (F9), and then press Return. This converts the cell entry to a true label, allowing you to format it with the /Range Label command options—unless the resulting string happens to be composed of only numeric values. In that case, pressing Edit (F2), Calc (F9), and Return converts the formula to a true value that is right-justified and can be used in other formula calculations.

EXAMPLE

If cell F5 contains the part number 101-AH-04567 and you need only the first three digits copied into cell P5, enter the following formula in cell P5:

@LEFT(F5,3)

The function displays 101 in P5. If you then press F2, F9, and Return, Lotus 1-2-3 enters the value 101 in the cell.

@LENGTH

The String Length Function

The @LENGTH function returns the number of characters contained in the string specified as its argument.

SYNTAX

@LENGTH(*string*)

where *string* is any character string entered between a pair of quotation marks or is a reference to a cell that contains a label entry.

USAGE

When you use the @LENGTH function, the program returns the total number of characters in the string, including spaces between words. You can use the & operator to concatenate cells so that the @LENGTH function returns the combined length of more than a single string. These strings can be literal (enclosed in quotes), cell references, or range names assigned to single-cell ranges.

EXAMPLES

To determine the length of a label in cell A12, simply enter

@LENGTH(A12)

If cell A12 contains the label "Human Resources", the program returns the value 15, indicating that there are 15 characters in this title, including the space between the words.

To determine the combined length of this label and one in B12, enter

@LENGTH(A12&B12)

If the label in B12 contains the label "Accounting", the result of this calculation is 25.

@LOWER

The Lowercase String Function

The @LOWER function converts all of the letters in the string specified as its argument to lowercase.

SYNTAX

@LOWER(*string*)

where *string* is any character string entered between a pair of quotation marks or is a reference to a cell that contains a label entry.

EXAMPLES

To convert a label entry in G29, which contains the string Cost Plus 40%, to lowercase letters, move the pointer to the cell where you want the converted label to appear and enter

@LOWER(G29)

The function returns the label "cost plus 40%".

@MID

The Midstring Function

The @MID function searches a string from a specified position within that string and extracts the number of characters desired from within it.

SYNTAX

@MID(*string,start number,n*)

where *string* is the overall string that contains the characters to be extracted (the substring), *start number* marks the position in the string where the search is to begin, and *n* is the number of characters in the substring to be extracted.

The *string* argument can be supplied by entering the string enclosed in quotation marks or by entering a cell reference to the cell containing the string. The *start number* and *n* arguments can be entered as values or as references to cells containing such values. The start number is computed from 0, marking the position of the first character, and increased by one for every character to the right.

USAGE

The @MID function allows you to extract (copy) a substring from a string by specifying the beginning position and the number of characters to be extracted. It is used whenever the substring characters to be reused are not located at the beginning of the string (where the @LEFT function is used) or the end of the string (where the @RIGHT function is used).

Because @MID requires the starting position, which is often unknown, as one of its arguments, you can effectively combine @MID with @FIND, which calculates the start position for you (see the examples that follow).

If the start number specified is a negative number or is greater than the number of positions in the string (equal to one less than the number of characters in the string), the function returns an ERR value. If the start number is entered as a mixed number, Lotus 1-2-3 uses only the integer portion of the number. Lotus 1-2-3 returns the specified number of characters from the overall string as a left-justified label.

EXAMPLES

To extract only a portion of a date entered as a label in the format MM-DD-YY, such as 11-23-89, you can use the @MID function. For instance, if you want only the day portion of such a date entered in cell S34, enter the formula

@MID(S34,3,2)

where 3 is the start position of the day value and 2 is the number of characters to be extracted.

However, if you are extracting days from such date labels and some of them were entered with single digits for the month (as in 2-13-90), specifying a start number of 3 will return the wrong characters. You can construct a formula that locates the day regardless of whether the month was entered with one or two digits:

@MID(S34,@FIND("-",S34,0) + 1,2)

This formula locates the position of the first hyphen and then uses this value plus one to locate the day and extract it.

@N

The Value Conversion String Function

The @N function returns the value of the first cell of the range specified as its argument.

SYNTAX

@N(*range*)

where *range* is a cell range designated by cell address or range name. This function returns the value of only the first cell (the one in the upper left corner) of a range composed of multiple cells. A single-cell range can also be specified. If the range consists of only a single cell, you can enter the address of that cell and Lotus 1-2-3 will automatically convert it into a cell range for you. For instance, it converts A3 to A3..A3.

USAGE

The @N function returns a value of 0 for the first cell in a cell range if the cell contains a string. It is used in error-trapping routines to prevent ERR values that would otherwise occur if calculations between strings and values were attempted.

EXAMPLE

To convert the contents of cells C3 and C4 to their numerical values and ensure that no ERR value can occur when they are added together, enter

@N(C3) + @N(C4)

in the cell where you want their sum. If C3 contained the label Price and C4 contained 105.45, the result would be 105.45 instead of the ERR value because the value in C3 was returned as 0 by the @N function.

@PROPER

The Proper Name String Function

The @PROPER function converts to uppercase only the initial letters of words separated by spaces in the string specified as its argument.

SYNTAX

@PROPER(*string*)

where *string* is any character string entered between a pair of quotation marks or is a reference to a cell that contains a label entry.

USAGE

The @PROPER function capitalizes initial letters of alphabetic strings and any letters separated by nonalphabetic characters. The program will copy the string, converting initial letters in each word to uppercase, regardless of the capitalization used when the original string was entered.

EXAMPLES

@PROPER regards nonalphabetic characters (numbers and symbols) as delimiters between words. For example, @PROPER converts

123-x

to

123-X

It converts

intro 12a

to

Intro 12A

To use @PROPER to convert a label entry in B12 containing the string "california consolidated", move the pointer to the cell where you want the converted label to appear and enter

@PROPER(B12)

It returns the label California Consolidated.

You can also use the & operator to have the program do this kind of conversion and join more than a single label. If B12 contains the label FIXED ASSETS, you can join it to the label in D12 with this formula:

@PROPER(B12&" - "&D12)

The formula produces the label California Consolidated - Fixed Assets.

@REPEAT

The Repeat String Function

The @REPEAT function repeats a specified string a specified number of times.

SYNTAX

@REPEAT(*string,n*)

where *string* is any character string entered between a pair of quotation marks or is a reference to a cell that contains a label entry, and *n* is the number of times those characters are to be repeated.

USAGE

The use of this function differs from that of a repeating label. When you use a repeating label, the characters are repeated until they fill the entire width of the cell. When you use the @REPEAT function, the characters are repeated as many times as indicated by the value supplied as the *n* argument. The characters may spill into the cells on the right if those cells are empty.

The @REPEAT function can be used to repeat any printable character, including special mathematical, graphics, or foreign-language symbols included in the LICS codes. To repeat one or more of these special characters, use the @CHAR function as the string argument of the @REPEAT function.

EXAMPLES

To repeat the characters - and * five times in cell A15 using the @REPEAT function, enter

@REPEAT("-"&"*",5)

This produces the following string of symbols:

```
-*-*-*-*-*
```

If the column width of column A were 9, one of these characters would be displayed in cell B15 if it were blank.

@REPLACE

The Replace String Function

The @REPLACE function locates a specific position in a string and replaces the desired number of characters with the new string specified as its last argument.

SYNTAX

@REPLACE(*original string,start number,n,new string*)

where *original string* is enclosed in quotation marks or is a reference to the cell that contains the string to be replaced. The *start number* is the value that marks the first position where the replacement is to be made. It is counted from 0 as the leftmost character in the original string. The *n* argument marks the number of characters to be replaced. The *new string* argument contains the replacement characters or a reference to the cell that contains the characters.

USAGE

The @REPLACE function adds a new substring to an original string, creating a new label. It can be used to replace part of a label and add new text to it. Only the number of characters indicated as the *n* argument will actually be deleted, even though all characters in the new string argument will be added at the position indicated by the value of the start number.

Because this function requires the starting position, which is often unknown, as one of its arguments, you can effectively combine @REPLACE with @FIND, which calculates this start position for you (see the examples that follow).

If the start number specified is a negative number or is greater than the number of positions in the string (equal to one less than the number of characters in the string), the function returns an ERR value. If the start number is entered as a mixed number, Lotus 1-2-3 uses only the integer portion of the number.

EXAMPLES

To use @REPLACE to amend a label in cell A5 that contains the text "Profits" so that it reads "After-Tax Profits", enter

@REPLACE(A5,0,0,"After-Tax")

The following @REPLACE function locates the position of the first hyphen in a date entered as a label in the format MM-DD in cell E20 and replaces it with the slash:

@REPLACE(E20,@FIND("-",E20,0),1,"/")

If the label in E20 contains the date 4-24, it is converted to 4/24 in the cell where this function is entered. The @FIND function automatically locates the position of the hyphen in E20, which is then the only character replaced in the string.

@RIGHT

The Right String Function

The @RIGHT function extracts the designated number of characters from the end of the specified string.

SYNTAX

@RIGHT(*string,n*)

where *string* is any character string entered between a pair of quotation marks or is a reference to a cell that contains a label entry, and *n* is the number of characters to be extracted from the end of the string.

USAGE

When you use the @RIGHT function, the number of characters extracted is counted from right to left from the end of the string, according to the value supplied as the n argument.

The program will copy the specified number of characters starting from the end of the string into the cell; they will be left-justified in the cell, like any label. However, the literal contents of the cell will be the formula @RIGHT(*string,n*). To convert this formula to a label entry, press the Edit (F2) key, followed by Calc (F9) and Return. This converts the cell entry to a true label that you can format with the /Range Label command options, unless the resulting string happens to be composed of only numeric values. In that case, pressing Edit (F2), Calc (F9), and Return converts the formula to a true, right-justified value that can be used in other formula calculations.

EXAMPLES

To extract only the last three characters from cell T8 containing the label "+2.4%", use the @RIGHT function as follows:

@RIGHT(T8,3)

It produces the label ".4%" in the cell where this function was entered.

@S

The String Value Function

The @S function returns the value of the first cell of the range specified as its argument as a string value.

SYNTAX

@S(*range*)

where *range* is a cell range designated by cell address or range name. This function returns the value of only the first cell (the one in the upper-left corner) of a range composed of multiple cells. A single-cell range can also be specified. If the range consists of a single cell, you can enter only the address of that cell; Lotus 1-2-3 automatically converts it into a cell range for you. For instance, it converts A3 to A3..A3.

USAGE

The @S function returns a null string value for the first cell in a cell range if the cell contains a value. It is used in error-trapping routines to prevent ERR values that would otherwise occur if calculations between values and strings were attempted.

EXAMPLES

To ensure that a concatenation between the strings in cells H7 and H8 could not result in an ERR value regardless of their contents, enter the formula

@S(H7)&" "&@S(H8)

in the cell where you want the labels joined. If cell H7 contains the label "After-Tax" and cell H8 contains the value 0.33, the result is simply the label "After-Tax". If cell H7 contains the value 5.67 and H8 contains the label "Profits", the result is "Profits" preceded by a single space. If cell H7 and H8 both contain values, the cell appears blank, even though it contains a single space. Under no conditions is the result an ERR value, as could easily be the case if the @S function were not used.

@STRING

The String Conversion Function

The @STRING function converts the numerical value specified as its *x* argument into a string.

SYNTAX

@STRING(*x*,*n*)

where *x* is the value or the cell reference to the value to be converted into a string, and *n* is the number of decimal places to be displayed. The @STRING function uses the Fixed format when converting a value to a string. The original value is rounded in the resulting string if the value of the *n* argument is less than the number of decimal places it contains.

USAGE

When you use the @STRING function, Lotus 1-2-3 returns a left-justified label containing the numeric string. If you want the label justified in some other way, you must add the appropriate number of spaces by concatenating them. (You cannot use the Edit (F2) and Calc (F9) keys, because they will convert the string back into a value.)

EXAMPLES

To convert the value 3.456 in cell K26 to a string value displaying only one decimal place, enter

@STRING(K26,1)

Lotus 1-2-3 returns the label "3.5" in the cell where you enter this function.

To convert the same value in cell K26 to a string displaying a percent sign, amend this formula to

@STRING(K26,1)&"%"

which produces the label "3.5%".

@TRIM

The Trim String Function

This function trims all preceding, trailing, and extra spaces from the specified string. The resulting string will still contain single spaces between words.

SYNTAX

@TRIM(*string*)

where *string* is any character string entered between a pair of quotation marks or is a reference to a cell that contains a label entry.

USAGE

This function can be used whenever you need to remove extraneous spaces from a label in the worksheet. It is especially useful in those situations where your data is imported with preceding spaces that must be removed. It relieves you of the tedious task of manually editing each label to delete the preceding spaces.

EXAMPLES

To remove the extraneous spaces from cell B2, which contains the string

Consumer   Deposits   and   Loans

enter this @TRIM function:

@TRIM(B2)

It returns the string

Consumer Deposits and Loans

properly spaced in cell B2.

@UPPER

The Uppercase String Function

The @UPPER function converts all letters in the specified string to uppercase.

SYNTAX

@UPPER(*string*)

where *string* is any character string entered between a pair of quotation marks or is a reference to a cell that contains a label entry.

EXAMPLES

To convert an entry made in all lowercase letters in cell G145 to uppercase, enter

@UPPER(G145)

If cell G145 contains the label "ny", the label in the cell where this function was entered will be NY. To convert the formula to a true label, you could then press the Edit key (F2), the Calc key (F9), and Return.

@VALUE

The @VALUE function converts the string specified as its argument into a value that can be included in calculations.

SYNTAX

@VALUE(*string*)

where *string* is a numerical string enclosed in quotes or is a cell reference to such a string.

USAGE

The @VALUE function can be used anytime you want to convert a string containing numeric values into values that can be used in mathematical calculations. Lotus 1-2-3 returns a value as long as the string indicated as its argument is expressed in one of the following formats:

- A label made up of all integers, such as 1345
- A label made up of decimal values, such as 17.678
- A label made up of fractions, such as 3 7/8
- A label using scientific notation, such as 1.24E3

The program returns an ERR value if the string contains comma delimiters, dollar signs, percent signs, or other such characters. You must add these by using the /Range Format command and the appropriate format.

EXAMPLES

To convert the label in cell R30 containing 5 7/16 to a value that can be used in calculation, enter

@VALUE(R30)

Lotus 1-2-3 returns the value 5.4375 in the cell where the function is entered.

To add two strings, one entered as 12.5 in R2 and the other entered as 3/8 in D2, enter

@VALUE(R2) + @VALUE(D2)

The program enters the calculated result 12.875 in the cell where this formula is entered.

17

Special Functions

The special functions represent a diverse group of functions that fall into three main subgroups:

- The lookup functions, @VLOOKUP, @HLOOKUP, and @INDEX, which retrieve values from lookup tables, and @CHOOSE and @@, which do not.
- The attribute functions. These include @COLS and @ROWS, which return the number of columns and rows in a cell range, and @CELL and @CELLPOINTER, which allow you to obtain information about specific attributes of a cell such as its position, contents, display format, label prefix, and so on.
- The special numerical values of @NA and @ERR. These allow you to input the special values of NA for not available and ERR for error.

@@
The Indirect Reference Function

The @@ function allows you to use the contents of a cell by indirect reference. Its argument contains a cell reference from which the program extracts the entry.

SYNTAX

@@(*cell address*)

where *cell address* is entered as a cell address or a range name given to a single-cell range. This cell reference must itself contain a single-cell range name, a cell address entered as a label, or a string formula whose result is either a cell address or a single-cell range name; otherwise, the @@ function will return an ERR value.

USAGE

The argument of the @@ function contains another cell reference entered either as a range name, or a cell address. The @@ function uses this cell reference as its lookup value and retrieves its contents in the cell where the @@ function is used.

The @@ function's argument can be either the literal label name of another cell, such as 'B10, a range name, or a cell address label in the input cell. To look up another item of data, you simply change the range name or cell address label in the input cell. If the cell referenced in the argument does not contain a valid cell address or range name entered as a label, you will receive an ERR value.

EXAMPLES

The following @@ function returns the value 110, stored in AA20, when the label 'AA20 is entered in cell A5:

@@(A5)

The following @@ function returns the label After-tax Income, stored in cell AB105, when the label 'AB105 is entered in cell A10:

@@(A10)

@CELL

The Cell Attribute Function

The @CELL function returns specific information about one particular attribute of the first cell in a cell range. Depending upon the attribute specified, you can obtain information about its contents, location, protection status, or width.

SYNTAX

@CELL(*attribute,range*)

where *attribute* is either "address", "row", "col", "contents", "type", "prefix", "protect", "width", or "format", or a cell reference to a cell containing one of these labels; and *range* is a cell range. The *range* argument can be specified by entering the cell addresses or range name, or by the pointing method.

If a single-cell range is used, you can preface it with an exclamation point to indicate it or enter just the single-cell address. If a multiple-cell range is used, the function will return information about the attribute argument specified only for the cell in the upper left corner of the range.

USAGE

The @CELL function is used to return a specific item of information about a particular cell in the spreadsheet, referred to as an attribute.

When you make a change to the cell or its contents that affects the type of attribute information returned by the @CELL function, it is not always automatically updated. (When "contents" is the attribute and you enter a new entry in the cell, this is immediately updated.) To have the @CELL formula reflect the change you have made, you must sometimes press the Calc key (F9).

EXAMPLES

If cell A10 contains the label Income, right-justified in the cell, and the cell width has been widened to 12 characters, any of the following could be used as arguments of the @CELL function:

@CELL("address",A10)

returns A10. Entering

@CELL("contents",A10)

returns Income. Entering

@CELL("type",A10)

returns l for label. Entering

@CELL("width",A10)

returns 12. Entering

@CELL("prefix",A10)

returns " for right justified.

@CELLPOINTER

The Cell Pointer Attribute Function

The @CELLPOINTER function returns specific information about one particular attribute of the current cell. Depending upon the attribute specified, you can obtain information about its contents, location, protection status, or width.

SYNTAX

@CELLPOINTER(*attribute*)

where *attribute* is either "address", "row", "col", "contents", "type", "prefix", "protect", "width", or "format", or a cell reference to a cell containing one of these labels.

USAGE

The @CELLPOINTER function is similar to the @CELL function, except that it returns attribute information about only the cell currently holding the cell pointer.

When the @CELLPOINTER function is first entered in a cell of the worksheet, it describes the type of attribute for the cell where the @CELLPOINTER function is used. As the cell pointer is moved to different cells in the spreadsheet, the cell containing the @CELLPOINTER function is updated only when a new entry is made in the spreadsheet. To update the attribute information when the cell pointer is located in a cell that already contains data, you must press the Calc key (F9).

Likewise, when used in macro commands, the @CELLPOINTER function is not automatically updated as the cell pointer is moved to different cells in the worksheet. Thus, you may have to include the commands {CALC} or {RECALC} when you need to have the function return new information about a particular attribute of a new current cell.

EXAMPLES

When entering **@CELLPOINTER("contents")** in a cell, with the "contents" attribute as the argument, the function returns the value 0 in the cell where this function is entered.

If the cell pointer is then moved to a new cell that contains the value 675, and you press the Calc key (F9), the program returns the value 675 in the cell that holds this function.

When entering **@CELLPOINTER("type")** in a cell, with the "type" attribute as the argument, the function returns v (for value) in the cell where the function is entered. If you move the cell pointer to a cell that contains the label Payment and you press the Calc key (F9), the program returns l (for label).

@CHOOSE

The Choose Function

The @CHOOSE function returns the value (or label if you are using Release 2) in the list of arguments that coincides with the offset value given as its first argument.

SYNTAX

@CHOOSE(*x,v0,v1,...,vn*)

where *x* is the number of the offset of the value to be returned, and *v0, v1,...,vn* form the list of possible values.

The *x* argument can be entered as a value or cell reference to a value that corresponds to the offset of the value to be used. If the *x* argument exceeds the value of the last offset or is a negative number, the function will return an ERR value. If the *x* argument contains a mixed number, the function will use only the integer portion as the offset. For example, an *x* argument of 0.5 will use the offset value of 0, 2.5 will use 2, and so on.

The value arguments can contain a list of entries or cell references (by cell address or range name). These arguments can consist of either strings or values. All strings must be enclosed in quotation marks when they are entered in the list of value arguments.

USAGE

The @CHOOSE function allows you to enter a list of lookup values without requiring that you set up a separate lookup table in the worksheet.

EXAMPLE

You can use the @CHOOSE function to return the weekday. In the following example, the day of the week is entered in cell A2 and the @CHOOSE function uses it to return the correct weekday.

@CHOOSE(A2 – 1,"Monday","Tuesday","Wednesday", "Thursday","Friday","Saturday","Sunday")

To obtain the weekday Sunday, enter 7 in cell A2. Because the offset of Sunday is 6, the function subtracts one from the value entered in cell A2.

@COLS

The Columns Function

The @COLS function returns the number of columns contained in the range of cells specified as its argument.

SYNTAX

@COLS(*range*)

where *range* is a cell range defined by cell addresses or range name. You can specify the range argument by typing in the cell addresses or by pointing to it.

USAGE

The @COLS function can help you indirectly determine the width of a particular cell range. By knowing the number of columns in the range, you can approximate the width in characters by estimating the average column width in the cell (often with the @CELL function using the "width" attribute) and multiplying that value by the number of columns returned by the @COLS function.

EXAMPLES

If you have a cell range named DATA and you want to estimate its width for printing, the following formula will return its approximate width in characters:

@COLS(DATA) * @CELL("width",DATA)

If the range named DATA extends from cells X12..AF90 and the cell width of X12 is 13, this formula returns the value 117 in the cell where it is entered.

The ERR Value Function

The @ERR function returns the ERR value, indicating the presence of an error in the cell where it is entered.

SYNTAX

```
@ERR
```

This function takes no argument.

USAGE

The @ERR function is usually included as part of an @IF formula to introduce an ERR value only under particular conditions. For instance, if a calculated value is not to fall below a certain amount, you could set up a condition that evaluated the result and used the @ERR function to enter an ERR value into the cell if that result was less than you would allow.

ERR values introduced into a cell will cause all cells containing dependent formulas to show an ERR value. Most often, you will want to prevent the proliferation of such an ERR value to all of the dependent formulas. To trap the @ERR value, you can use the @ISERR function in the dependent formulas so that a value such as zero is returned whenever ERR is brought forward.

EXAMPLES

In the following formula, the program enters an ERR value if the calculated result in cell C50 ever falls below $10,000.00. Otherwise, it goes ahead and uses its value in the intended division by the value in D50.

```
@IF(C50<10000,@ERR,C50/D50)
```

NOTES

Lotus 1-2-3 will also automatically enter an ERR value into a cell whose calculation is not allowed under its rules of calculation. Most often, the cause of ERR values entered by the program is a calculation that calls for division by zero or the deletion of a necessary cell reference or range name. This ERR value introduced automatically by the program is identical to entering an ERR value with the @ERR function.

SEE ALSO

@ISERR

@HLOOKUP

The Horizontal Lookup Function

The @HLOOKUP function matches the value specified as its *x* argument against those listed in the first row of a lookup table whose extent is indicated in the *range* argument. It then returns the value listed in the row indicated by the row number argument in the column holding the matching value.

SYNTAX

@HLOOKUP(*x*,*range*,*row number*)

where *x* is the selector value that is to be matched in the first row of the lookup table, *range* is the range of cells that contains all of the values in the lookup table, and *row number* indicates the row offset used to return the value.

The *x* or *range* argument can be indicated by cell addresses or range name. Row offsets are counted from zero from the first row of the range. The row offset argument is usually entered as a value, although it can also contain a reference to a cell that contains the appropriate row offset number.

USAGE

The @HLOOKUP table is used to automatically retrieve values from a horizontal lookup table located in the same spreadsheet. This lookup function is data dependent in that it uses a selector value to locate the appropriate value to be retrieved.

In the horizontal arrangement, the index column against which a selector value is matched is the first row of the lookup table. The program matches this value against those listed in this row, moving from the first cell of the range to the right.

When an exact match is located, the value in the column that corresponds to the row offset number is entered in the cell where the function is entered. If no exact match is located in the table, the program stops at the column holding the next highest value and then moves back to the previous column. Once this column is located, the row offset is used to select the appropriate value.

In Release 2, the selector value and values in the lookup table can contain strings (labels) as well as numeric values. If you are using Release 1A, both the selector value and all the values in the lookup tables must consist of numeric values.

EXAMPLE

Figure 17.1 shows how the @HLOOKUP function finds a match for the selector values and chooses the appropriate value.

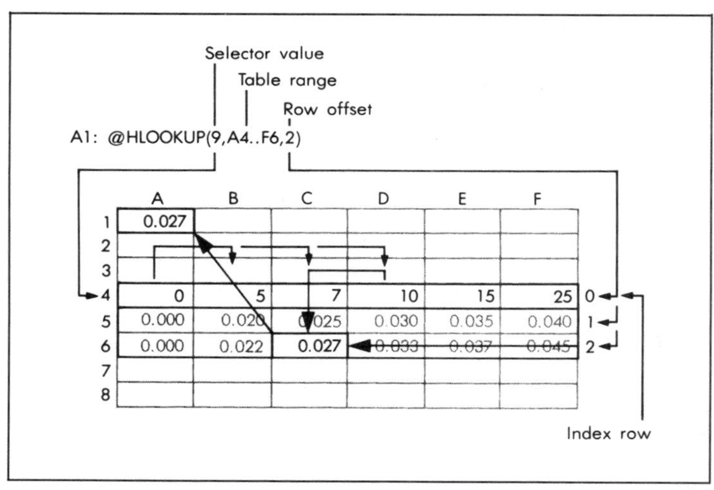

Figure 17.1: The @HLOOKUP function

@INDEX

The Index Function

The @INDEX function returns the value from the lookup table indicated by the range argument. The value is specified by the column and row offsets included as the function's column and row arguments.

SYNTAX

@INDEX(*range,column,row*)

where *range* is the range of cells containing all of the lookup values, *column* is the column offset number, and *row* is the row offset number.

The range can be indicated by cell addresses or range name. Column and row offsets are counted from zero from the first cell of the range (the one in the upper left corner of the range), so that this cell has a column and row offset of zero.

If the values for the column or row offsets are negative or exceed the total number of offsets, the function returns an ERR value. If a mixed number is used as either offset value, the program uses only the integer portion.

USAGE

The @INDEX function retrieves a particular value from a lookup table located in the same spreadsheet. The @INDEX function retrieves the appropriate value by its position in the table alone. Therefore, it requires that you enter both the column and row offset as arguments.

EXAMPLE

Figure 17.2 shows how the @INDEX function selects the appropriate value by using the column and row offset numbers.

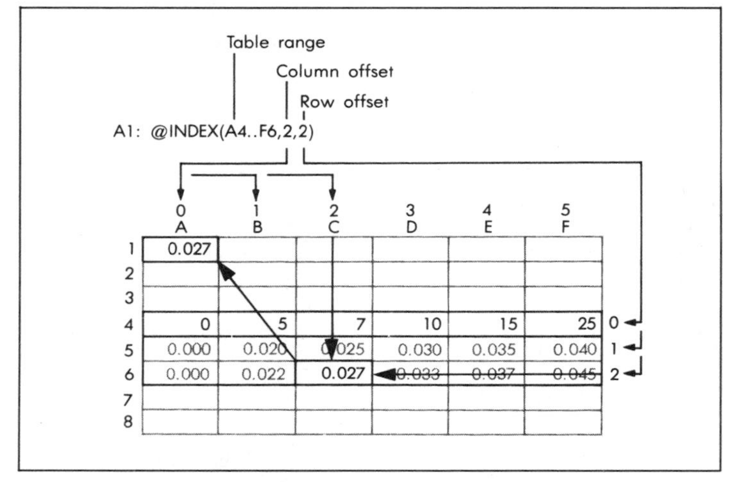

Figure 17.2: The @INDEX function

@NA

The NA Value Function

The @NA function returns the NA value, indicating that a value is not available in the cell where it is entered.

SYNTAX

@NA

This function takes no argument.

USAGE

The @NA function is used to introduce the notation NA (for not available) in any cell that still requires data that you do not yet have. When you use it, it enters this notation as a special value that is then brought forward to any other cell that contains a formula whose calculation depends upon its value. As soon as you replace the NA value with a value and recalculate the spreadsheet, all NA values in those cells will be replaced by their corrrectly calculated values.

EXAMPLE

To alert yourself that the input cell B4 does not yet contain a required value, enter the following formula to calculate the total in cell B24:

@IF(B4=0,@NA,@SUM(B4..B22))

SEE ALSO

@ISNA

@ROWS

The Rows Function

The @ROWS function returns the number of rows contained in the range of cells specified as its argument.

SYNTAX

@ROWS(*range*)

where *range* is a cell range defined by cell addresses or range name. The range argument may be specified by typing in the cell addresses or by pointing to it.

USAGE

Use of the @ROWS function is similar to that of the @COLS function, and they are often used together to determine the overall size of a particular cell range in the spreadsheet. Because rows cannot be widened or narrowed, the value returned by the @ROWS function always tells you the exact line length of the range.

To determine the number of cells in a particular range, multiply the number of columns by the number of rows as follows:

@COLS(*range*)*@ROWS(*range*)

Enter the *range* by cell addresses or range name.

EXAMPLE

If you name the cell range A6..E16 PrintBlock and enter the formula

@ROWS(PrintBlock)

Lotus 1-2-3 returns the value 11 in the cell where this formula is entered.

@VLOOKUP

The Vertical Lookup Function

The @VLOOKUP function matches the value specified as its *x* argument against those listed in the first column of a lookup table whose extent is indicated in the range argument. It then returns the value listed in the column indicated by the column number argument in the row holding the matching value.

SYNTAX

@VLOOKUP(*x,range,column number*)

where *x* is the value that is to be matched in the first column of the lookup table, *range* is the range of cells that contains all of the values in the lookup table, and *column number* indicates the column offset used to return the value.

The *range* argument can be indicated by cell addresses or range name. Column offsets are counted from zero from the first column of the range.

USAGE

The @VLOOKUP table is used to retrieve values automatically from a vertical lookup table located in the same spreadsheet. This lookup function is data dependent in that it uses a selector value to locate the appropriate value to be retrieved.

In the vertical arrangement, the index column against which a particular value is matched is the first column of the lookup table. The program matches this value against values listed in this column, moving from the first cell of the range down.

When an exact match is located, the value in the row that corresponds to the column offset number is entered in the cell where the function is entered. If no exact match is located in the table, the program stops at the row holding the next highest value and then moves up to the previous row. Once this row is located, the column offset is used to select the appropriate value.

In Release 2, the selector value and values in the lookup table can contain strings (labels) as well as numeric values. If you are using Release 1A, both the selector value and all values in the lookup tables must consist of numeric values.

EXAMPLE

Figure 17.3 shows how the @VLOOKUP function finds a match for the selector values and chooses the appropriate value.

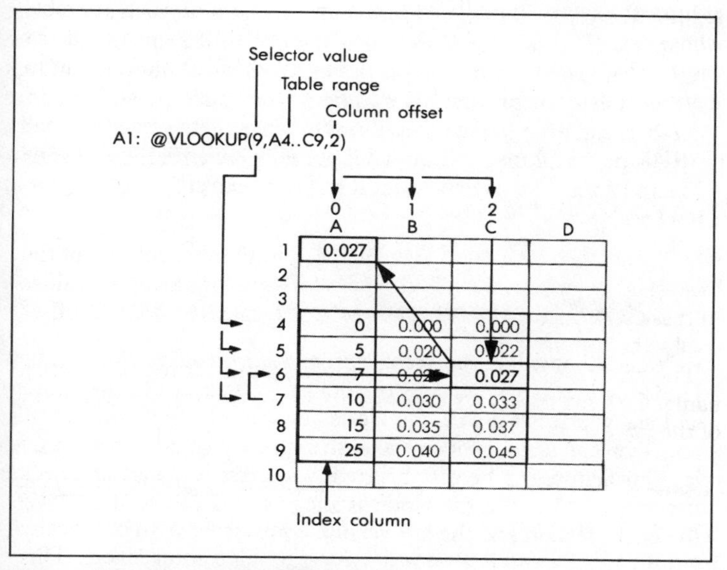

Figure 17.3: The @VLOOKUP function

Important New Features of Release 2.2

Lotus 1-2-3 Release 2.2 contains several new and exciting features. You can now instantly recover from mistakes, such as deleting a large section of your worksheet. You can now print much more complicated and interesting documents. 1-2-3 will now let you link spreadsheets, incorporating numbers from one spreadsheet into another, and even update these links to make them current. Finally, 1-2-3's powerful macro commands are now enhanced with the new Macro Library Manager add-in. It lets you keep groups of macros in libraries.

Undo: Recovering from Disaster

Release 2.2 now lets you recover from your mistakes with the new Undo feature. It saves a copy of your entire spreadsheet in memory and lets you recall it with the Undo key, Alt-F4, if you make a mistake. You can actually erase the entire spreadsheet and then recover it. This feature can be very handy if you make a change and decide not to use it. You can use Undo as a toggle; you can switch between the latest version and the last version by pressing Alt-F4.

KEY SEQUENCE

Alt-F4

Once you press Alt-F4, the spreadsheet immediately reverts to its previous state.

NOTE

With the power of Undo comes a major drawback: it consumes a great deal of your computer's memory. If you work with large spreadsheets, you might need to disable Undo; use the command **/WGDOUD**. Then type **/WGDU** to update your settings file if you want to permanently disable Undo.

The Allways Add-In: A Better Way to Print

With Release 2.2, Lotus provides Allways, a printing program that was previously distributed by Funk software. Allways can format numbers and text, combine numbers with text and graphs, scale graphs, place headers and footers on your printouts, and produce lines and shading. Allways gives you the power to create exciting presentation graphics.

Allways is an add-in program and must be attached before it can be invoked. To attach it, select /Add-In Attach, select ALLWAYS, and choose a key for it or enter **N** for No-Key. Next, press the key you selected, or enter **/Add-In Invoke** if you selected No-Key. You will see a screen that is similar to Lotus 1-2-3. First, you can move around this screen with all the normal keys. Second, you reach the menus by pressing **/**, just as in 1-2-3. Finally, many of the menu options are similar to those of the 1-2-3 main menu. The Allways main menu contains the following items:

Worksheet Format Graph Layout Print Display Special Quit

Note, however, that there are some important differences between 1-2-3 and Allways:

- You cannot enter numbers or formulas in Allways.
- When you want to change a range of columns or rows in 1-2-3, you select the command and then choose the range. In Allways, you often select the range and then choose the action. Use the . (period) key to anchor a range and then select cells by moving the arrow keys.
- You cannot use Allways without a hard disk.

- You cannot edit data in Allways; you must switch back to 1-2-3 by pressing Esc or **/Q**.
- Allways supports a somewhat different range of printers than 1-2-3; check the Allways section of the Lotus documentation to make sure your printer will work.
- Allways assigns different meanings to some function keys and also includes special Alt-key combinations known as *accelerator keys* (see Tables A.1 and A.2).
- If you do not have a graphics display adapter to see the contents of a graph in Allways, you must use F6 to switch the display to text mode.

Table A.1: The Allways Function Keys

Key	Name	Usage
F1	Help	Gives you online, context-sensitive help.
F3	Name	Displays a list of range names or file names, depending on the command.
F4	Reduce	Reduces the size of the Allways display by cycling through the same sizes as offered by the Tiny, Small, Normal, Large, and Huge options on the /Display Zoom menu.
Shift-F4	Enlarge	Enlarges the size of the Allways display by cycling through the same sizes as offered by the Tiny, Small, Normal, Large, and Huge options on the /Display Zoom menu.
F5	Goto	Moves the pointer to a specific cell address (can be used with range names specified by the Name key, as in 1-2-3).
F6	Display	Switches the Allways display between graphics and text modes.
F10	Graph	Turns the display of a 1-2-3 graph brought into an Allways report on and off. When the display is off, the graph is represented by a shaded box that indicates its position on the page.

Table A.2: The Allways Accelerator Keys

Key	Usage
Alt-1	Selects Font 1
Alt-2	Selects Font 2
Alt-3	Selects Font 3
Alt-4	Selects Font 4
Alt-5	Selects Font 5
Alt-6	Selects Font 6
Alt-7	Selects Font 7
Alt-8	Selects Font 8
Alt-B	Toggles bold on or off
Alt-G	Toggles grid lines on or off
Alt-L	Selects lines: outline, all, or none
Alt-S	Selects shades: light, dark, solid, or none
Alt-U	Selects underline: single, double, or none

The following sections discuss each submenu on the Allways main menu; this menu is assumed as the starting point of each key sequence.

The /Worksheet Menu

This menu allows you to set the sizes of rows and columns, as well as insert page breaks exactly where you want them.

OPTIONS

- Column
- Row
- Page

The /Worksheet Column Command

KEY SEQUENCE

/WC *<S/R>*

OPTIONS

- Set-Width: sets the width of a column range.
- Reset-Width: returns the column width to the value set in Lotus 1-2-3.

The /Worksheet Row Command

KEY SEQUENCE

/WR *<S/A>*

OPTIONS

- Set-Height: specifies the height in points of a row or group of rows.
- Auto: has Allways automatically set the height of a row, depending upon the height of text in that row.

The /Worksheet Page Option

This command inserts page breaks at specified points in your spreadsheet. This can help you control how your spreadsheet looks when you print it, even though it might be very large.

KEY SEQUENCE

/WP *<R/C/D>*

OPTIONS

- Row: starts a new page at a certain row in your spreadsheet.
- Column: starts a new page at a certain column in your spreadsheet.
- Delete: deletes a page break that you have inserted.

The /Format Menu

This menu lets you change the way numbers and text appear in your printed document.

OPTIONS

- Font
- Bold
- Underline
- Color
- Lines
- Shade
- Reset
- Quit

The /Format Font Command

This command controls all of the fonts used in your worksheet. It allows you to maintain several collections of fonts and substitute one font for another throughout the worksheet.

A *font* in Allways is a particular combination of type face (such as Courier, used on most typewriters, or Plantin, used in this book), style (such as *italic* or regular), and size, which is specified in points. Thus, Courier 10 point regular, Courier 10 point italic, and Courier 12 point regular are all different fonts. **Boldface** type is treated in Allways as an attribute that you specify independently of font.

A font *set* in Allways is a collection of up to eight fonts available for use at any given time. If your printer can produce more fonts, you can maintain a *library* of font sets.

KEY SEQUENCE

FF *<option>*

OPTIONS

- Use: selects a font from your font set to use in a specified cell or cell range of the worksheet.
- Replace: replaces one font in the available set with another, and substitutes the menu font wherever the old font was used in the worksheet.
- Default: either restores your font set to its default or updates it to make the current set the default.
- Library: maintains a library of font sets on disk, by either retrieving, saving, or deleting a specified set.

The /Format Bold Command

Use this command to make a cell or cell range stand out with a bold type style. It is also used to remove this bold style.

KEY SEQUENCE

/FB *<S/C>* *<range>*

OPTIONS

- Set: uses a bold type style on a range of cells.
- Clear: removes the bold effect from a range of cells.

The /Format Underline Command

This command underlines a cell range with either single or double underlining. It also removes underlining.

KEY SEQUENCE

/FU *<S/D/C>* *<range>*

OPTIONS

- Single: underlines a range of cells with a single underscore.
- Double: underlines a range of cells with a double underscore.
- Clear: removes underlining from a cell range.

The /Format Color Command

This command changes the color of a cell range.

KEY SEQUENCE

/FC *<color number>* *<range>*

OPTIONS

- 1: Black
- 2: Red
- 3: Green
- 4: Blue
- 5: Cyan
- 6: Magenta
- 7: White
- 8: Red-on-negs

The /Format Lines Command

Use this command to place lines or boxes around ranges of your spreadsheet. You can place grid lines around data, put a box around a cell or range, create summation lines, or even place vertical bars on either or both sides of a range.

KEY SEQUENCE

***/FL** <option> <range>*

OPTIONS

- Outline: surrounds a range with a box.
- Left: places vertical lines to the left of each cell in a range.
- Right: places vertical lines to the right of each cell in a range.
- Top: places horizontal lines above each cell in a range.
- Bottom: places horizontal lines below each cell in a range.
- All: places lines on all four sides of every cell in a range. This creates a grid pattern that makes a spreadsheet easier to read.
- Clear: clears the lines from one or all sides of a cell range. You can select Left, Right, Top, Bottom, or All.

The /Format Shade Command

This command lets you apply shading to a cell or cell range.

KEY SEQUENCE

***/FS** <L/D/S/C> <range>*

OPTIONS

- Light: applies a light shading to an area of your spreadsheet. (Text is still readable with this shading.)
- Dark: applies a dark shading to an area of your spreadsheet, which often makes text difficult to read.
- Solid: applies a solid shading to a range.
- Clear: removes shading from a range.

The /Format Reset Option

This command clears all formatting from a range and resets fonts to the default.

KEY SEQUENCE

/FR *<range>*

The /Graph Menu

This menu lets you control the way graphs are printed in your final document.

OPTIONS

- Add
- Remove
- Goto
- Settings
- Fonts-Directory

The /Graph Add Command

Use this command to include a graph in your printout. You can choose from all of the files in your program directory with the .PIC extension. You specify the position and size of the graph when you add it by specifying the range of the spreadsheet where you want the graph to appear. By default, Allways will display a box indicating the size and position of the graph. To see the contents of the graph, use F10 to switch to graph mode.

KEY SEQUENCE

/GA *<graph>* *<range>*

The /Graph Remove Command

This command removes a graph from your printout. You are given a choice of all the graphs in the current spreadsheet.

KEY SEQUENCE

/GR *<graph>*

The /Graph Goto Option

Use this command to locate the pointer in the first cell of the specified graph. This will place the graph in the upper-left corner of the screen.

KEY SEQUENCE

***/GG** <graph>*

The /Graph Settings Command

Use this command to change the appearance of a graph you have placed in your document.

KEY SEQUENCE

***/GS** <graph> <P/F/S/C/R/M/D> ...*

NOTE

If your pointer is not on a graph when you select /Graph Settings, Lotus will ask you which graph you want to modify. If your pointer is on a graph, you will be taken directly to the /Graph Settings screen, shown in Figure A.1.

OPTIONS

- PIC-File: changes the graph file that is included in your spreadsheet.
- Fonts: allows you to change the fonts for a graph. You can set the font for the first line of the title or for all other text in the graph.

```
GRAPH(1) D:\123R2-2\TEST.PIC                                                        MENU
PIC-File  Fonts  Scale  Colors  Range  Margins  Default  Quit
Replace a graph in the worksheet with a different graph file

   .PIC file: D:\123R2-2\TEST.PIC

   Fonts                                              Range: A1..C4
     1: BLOCK1      Scale: x 1.00
     2: BLOCK1      Scale: x 1.00

   Colors                                             Margins (in inches)
     X: Black                                             Left:   0.00
     A: Black                                            Right:   0.00
     B: Black                                              Top:   0.00
     C: Black                                           Bottom:   0.00
     D: Black
     E: Black
     F: Black

18
19
20
16-Aug-89  08:59 PM
```

Figure A.1: The /Graph Settings screen

- Scale: changes the scale of either font used in the current graph. This range of available scale factors is 0.5 to 3.
- Colors: lets you specify the color for each data range (X, A–F) on the graph. The available colors are listed under /Format Color in this appendix.
- Range: allows you to change the size and location of a graph by specifying the range of the spreadsheet where you want the graph to appear.
- Margins: sets the margins for a graph. The options (Left, Right, Top, Bottom) are analogous to those in 1-2-3's /Print Printer Options Margins command.
- Default: either restores the default settings to the current graph or saves the current settings as the new default.

The /Graph Fonts-Directory Option

Use this command to specify which directory will contain the font (.FNT) files to be used in printing the graphs. This is usually your Lotus 1-2-3 directory: C:\123, or C:\LOTUS.

KEY SEQUENCE

/GF *<directory>*

The /Layout Menu

This menu, illustrated in Figure A.2, lets you change the overall design of your printout. It gives you the ability to control page size, margins, headers, footers, and borders. It is useful in giving your reports a "finished" look.

OPTIONS

- Page-Size
- Margins
- Titles
- Borders
- Options
- Default
- Library
- Quit

The /Layout Page-Size Command

This command controls the size of the page you are using. The default is a standard 8½ × 11 sheet, but several other choices are

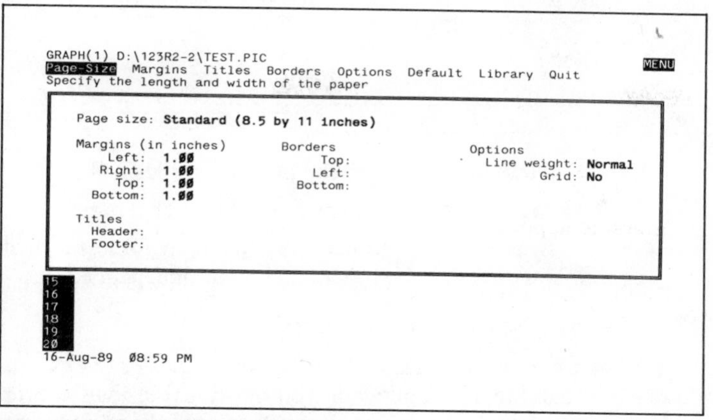

Figure A.2: The /Layout Menu

available. Your particular choices depend on your printer.

KEY SEQUENCE

/LP *<size>*

The /Layout Margins Command

Use this command to leave more white space around your report. Set a wider left margin if you are having your printout bound.

KEY SEQUENCE

/LM *<L/R/T/B>* *<margin>*

OPTIONS

- Left: sets the spacing for the left margin.
- Right: sets the spacing for the right margin.
- Top: sets the spacing for the top margin.
- Bottom: sets the spacing for the bottom margin.

The /Layout Titles Command

This command controls the headers and footers in your report. Headers and footers are discussed under /Print Options in Chapter 5.

KEY SEQUENCE

/LT *<option>*

OPTIONS

- Header: allows you to specify the header for your report.
- Footer: allows you to specify the footer for your report.
- Clear: lets you remove your headers and footers for less formal reports. You can clear the header and footer independently.

The /Layout Borders Command

This Allways command works in the same way as the /Print Options Border command in 1-2-3, allowing you to print title rows and/or columns on each page of a report. Even if you specify only certain cells within a row or column as your border, Allways (like 1-2-3) will print the entire row or column. You can specify more than one row or column as a border. Note that, as in 1-2-3, you must make sure not to include the same rows or columns in both the borders and the print range, or they will appear twice.

KEY SEQUENCE

/LB *<option>*

OPTIONS

- Top: analogous to the Rows option in /Print Options Border; lets you select a range of rows to be printed at the top of each page.
- Left: analogous to the Columns option in /Print Options Border; lets you select a range of columns to be printed on the left side of each page.
- Bottom: has no analogy in 1-2-3; lets you select a range of rows to be printed at the bottom of each page.
- Clear: deletes any borders specified by other options.

The /Layout Options Menu

The options on this menu allow you to control the thickness of all boxes, lines, and outlines (created with /Format Lines) used in your report, and to place or remove a grid of dotted lines between every cell of your worksheet. The grid is not affected by the Line-Weight option and can also be toggled on and off with Alt-G.

KEY SEQUENCE

/LO *<option>*

OPTIONS

- Line-Weight
- Grid

The /Layout Default Command

This command will either restore the default settings to the current layout or save the current settings as the new default.

KEY SEQUENCE

/LD *<R/U>*

OPTIONS

- Restore: recalls your default layout settings and makes them current.
- Update: saves your current layout settings and makes them the default.

The /Layout Library Command

Use this command to maintain several different layouts, which you can use for different spreadsheets. Simply recall them when you want to format a document a certain way. This can save you a lot of typing and make your documents uniform.

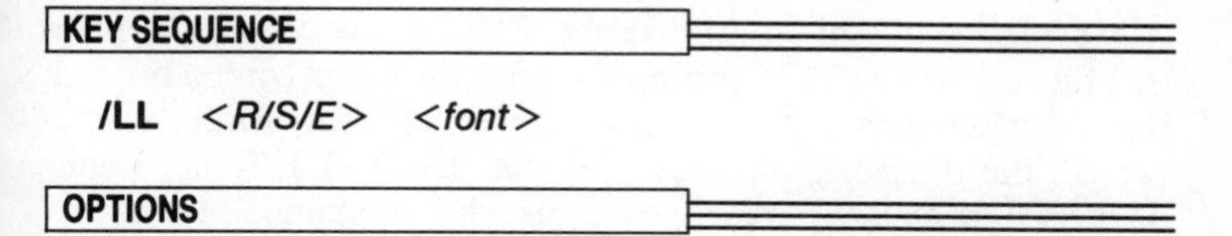

KEY SEQUENCE

/LL *<R/S/E>* *<font>*

OPTIONS

- Retrieve: loads a layout from disk. Allways will show you all of the layouts that have been saved. These files have the .ALS extension.

- Save: saves the current layout to disk, so it can be used again.
- Erase: deletes a layout from the disk.

The /Print Menu

This menu allows you to specify your printer setup and what you want to print, and then lets you print it.

KEY SEQUENCE

/P *<option>*

OPTIONS

- Go
- File
- Range
- Configuration
- Settings

The /Print Go Option

This command actually tells the printer to print. Use it after you have set up all of the other options on this menu, including printer and interface.

KEY SEQUENCE

/PG

The /Print File Command

Use this command to save your printout in a special file. Unlike the ASCII files you create with the /Print File command in 1-2-3, this file will contain exactly the same data that the printer would have received, including all graphics and printer codes. By default, Allways gives this file the extension .ENC (for encoded). To print this file, exit to the DOS prompt and use the Copy command with the /B switch. Specify the interface to which your printer is connected. For example, to print a file called BUDGET.ENC on your printer connected to parallel port 1, use the command:

```
COPY BUDGET.ENC/B LPT1:
```

/B is a special DOS option for binary files.

KEY SEQUENCE

/PF *<file>*

The /Print Range Option

Use this command to specify the range you want to print. You must define which area of your document you want to print before you select /Print Go.

KEY SEQUENCE

/PR *<S/C>* *<range>*

OPTIONS

- Set: selects the range you want to print and outlines your print range with dotted lines.
- Clear: clears the range you specified earlier, removing the dotted lines.

The /Print Configuration Command

This command displays the menu shown in Figure A.3. It allows you to specify the printer name and other relevant information.

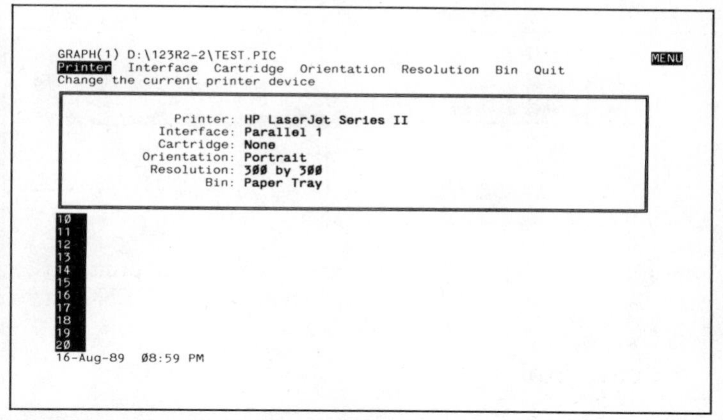

Figure A.3: The /Print Configuration menu

OPTIONS

- Printer: lets you specify the printer you are using. You can choose from all of the printers you configured when you installed Allways.
- Interface: lets you specify the interface, or port, where your printer is attached. If you select a serial printer, make sure you have set the speed (baud rate) with DOS's MODE command before you print.
- Cartridge: lets you select a font cartridge plugged into your laser printer.
- Orientation: lets you select the orientation of your printout, either vertical (portrait) or horizontal (landscape).
- Resolution: lets you change the resolution of your laser printer. Use this option to select a lower resolution if you get an out-of-memory error and cannot print a page.
- Bin: lets you select the bin or paper-feed method if your printer has more than one.

The /Print Settings Command

This command displays the menu shown in Figure A.4. It allows you to specify the first and last pages to be printed, the page numbering (that is, if you begin printing with, say, the third page of your spreadsheet, you can designate that as page 1 of your printout), and whether to

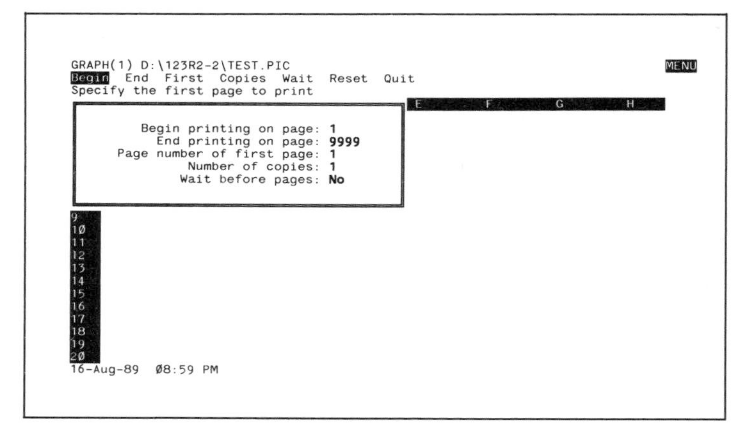

Figure A.4: The /Print Settings menu

pause between pages. You can also clear all of your settings to restore the defaults.

KEY SEQUENCE

/PS *<option>*

OPTIONS

- Begin: sets the first page that will be printed.
- End: sets the last page that will be printed.
- First: sets the page number of the first page to be printed.
- Copies: specifies how many copies of your document will be printed.
- Wait: stops your printer between pages when printing, so you can add more paper.
- Reset: clears all of the settings you specified and returns them to the default settings.

The /Display Menu

This menu lets you choose how your spreadsheet looks as you work on it. You can change the quality of the display you see as well as the colors and the magnification.

OPTIONS

- Mode
- Zoom
- Graphs
- Colors

The /Display Mode Command

This command lets you change the type of screen you see. By default, Allways uses graphics mode, where everything on the screen is drawn by Allways. This allows the display of text and graphics simultaneously, giving you a good display but poor performance. The alternative, text mode, can display only text. Lotus 1-2-3 uses text mode for everything but displaying graphs.

Figure A.5 shows the Display Mode menu.

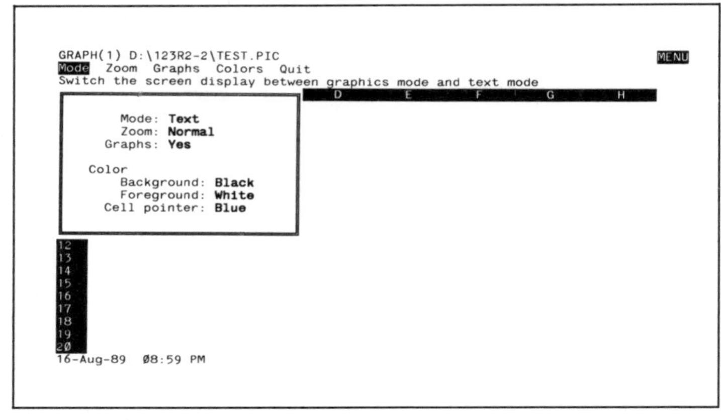

Figure A.5: The Display Mode menu

KEY SEQUENCE

/DM *<G/T>*

OPTIONS

- Graphics: displays graphs and text simultaneously.
- Text: displays text only.

The /Display Zoom Command

This command lets you see your spreadsheet at different magnifications. You can see a tiny part of it close-up or a large amount of it from far away.

KEY SEQUENCE

/DZ *<T/S/N/L/H>*

OPTIONS

- Tiny: shows a small part of your spreadsheet.
- Small: shows a larger part of your spreadsheet.

- Normal: shows the standard amount of your sheet.
- Large: shows an even bigger section of your spreadsheet.
- Huge: shows the largest portion of your spreadsheet.

The /Display Colors Command

Use this command to change the colors that you see while working on your spreadsheet. This command does not affect the colors that will be printed if you have a color printer or plotter; use /Format Color for that purpose.

KEY SEQUENCE

/DC *<B/F/C>*

OPTIONS

- Background: sets the color of the sheet itself.
- Foreground: changes the color of the text in your spreadsheet.
- Cell-Pointer: chooses the color of your pointer.

The /Special Menu

This menu lets you manipulate formats and settings as well as justify text.

OPTIONS

- Copy
- Move
- Justify
- Import

The /Special Copy Command

This command allows you to copy the format from one area of your spreadsheet and apply it to another area.

KEY SEQUENCE

/SC *<from range>* *<to range>*

The /Special Move Command

This command is similar to /Special Copy, but it resets the format of the *from* range to the default after making the move. Be careful when you use this command, because it moves the settings from the entire *from* range, even if you specify a smaller *to* range.

KEY SEQUENCE

/SM *<from range>* *<to range>*

The /Special Justify Command

This command will move text around within cells to make the text fit within a specified range as well as possible. It works in the same way as the /Range Justify command in 1-2-3. If you have entered text into a single column of cells, you can have Allways move your text around so that it fills a range.

KEY SEQUENCE

/SJ *<range>*

The /Special Import Command

Use this command to include the format and settings from another spreadsheet in your current spreadsheet. This feature can save you a lot of time by allowing you to recreate the look of another spreadsheet. Be careful when using this command, because you can lose a lot of work if you don't like the new settings.

KEY SEQUENCE

/SI *<spreadsheet>*

SEE ALSO

/Add-In Attach
/Add-In Invoke

Linking Worksheet Files

When your are building formulas in a Release 2.2 worksheet, 1-2-3 allows you to refer to data in any other worksheet file saved on disk. When you build a formula in a worksheet that refers to data in another file, you create a *link* between the two files. The file in which you enter the formula (that is, the current worksheet) is called the *target file*, and the file that contains the value referred to is called the *source file*. Once these files are linked, 1-2-3 copies the value of the cell in the source file (also known as the *source cell*) to the cell in the target file (also known as the *target cell*).

When creating a formula that refers to data in another file, you must follow this format:

+<<*file reference*>>*cell reference*

Note that this format only enables you bring forward the value of a source cell into a target cell. However, once it has been copied into the target file, you can include the target cell in any valid 1-2-3 formula.

Remember that the file reference contains the name of the file (including the extension) enclosed in double angle brackets, as in

+<<IS90CH5.WK1>>C12

If the worksheet file is not located in the current directory, the file reference must include the path name as well as the complete file name, as in

+<<C:\DATA\IS90CH5.WK1>>D5

The cell reference can be given by cell address or range name, if one has been assigned to the cell in the source file, as in

+<<C:\DATA\IS90CH5.WK1>>INCOME

Note that if you enter a range name that has been assigned to a range larger than one cell, 1-2-3 copies just the first cell of this range into the target cell.

If the file to which a formula refers doesn't exist in the directory specified by the file reference (or in the current directory, if the file reference doesn't specify the directory), or if the file is later deleted from the directory, the formula will return ERR in the worksheet.

When using Release 2.2 on a network and sharing linked files, you will want to use the /File Admin Link-Refresh command (**/FAL**) periodically to ensure than all links have been properly updated. You should always select /File Admin Link-Refresh before saving the worksheet.

The Macro Library Manager Add-In

This add-in program, which Lotus 1-2-3 now provides in Release 2.2, offers a new way to create and manage libraries of macros. You can save them in a file and in your computer's memory, edit them, and load them into any spreadsheet. The Macro Library Manager, nicknamed *Hyperspace*, enables you to store collections of macros in a special library file that resides not only on the disk but also in RAM. Once you load the library file into memory, you can use the macros it contains with any worksheet that you begin or retrieve during the work session. Hyperspace macros remain in memory independent of any particular worksheet. They occupy no cells and therefore have no cell addresses until you read them into a worksheet. Lotus 1-2-3 assigns the filename extension .MLB to all macro library files.

NOTE

You must attach the Macro Library Manager with the **/AA** command before you can use it. All key sequences in this section assume that you have attached this add-in to an Alt–function-key combination between F7 and F10.

OPTIONS

- Load
- Save
- Edit
- Remove
- Name-List

The Macro Manager Load Command

This command lets you load a macro library from disk into memory. Doing so doesn't read the macros into the spreadsheet, it just brings them into the Macro Library Manager. Macro libraries must be brought into memory before they can be edited with the Edit command.

KEY SEQUENCE

Alt-<*function key*> **L** <*library*> **[**<*Y/N*>**]**

If there isn't another library with the same name in memory, the library you choose will be loaded into memory. If there is a library with the same name in memory, you will be asked whether or not to overwrite it.

The Save Command

Use this command to store a macro or group of macros into memory and to disk. You can elect to assign a password (of up to 80 characters) to a file when you save it. This prevents other users from editing your macros, but not from loading them into their spreadsheets.

KEY SEQUENCE

Alt-*<function key>* **S** *<library>* **[***<Y/N>***]** *<range>* **[***<Y/N>***]** **[***<password>***]**

After you select the Save command, enter the name of the library you want to save. If a file with this name exists, you will be asked if you want to overwrite it. Next, specify the range that contains the macros you want to save. Finally, you will be asked if you want to protect this library with a password. If you do, type **Y** and enter a password.

The Edit Command

This command allows you to edit a library of macros that is stored in memory. It writes the contents of a library file from memory into the current spreadsheet.

NOTE

Be careful when specifying the range for the macro library; your macros could overwrite existing data.

KEY SEQUENCE

Alt-*<function key>* **E** *<library>* **[***<password>***]** *<I/O>* *<range>*

After you select the library you wish to edit, you will be prompted for a password if there was one assigned when it was saved. Next, you will be asked if you want to ignore new range names in the macro library you are editing that conflict with existing names. You can also choose to overwrite existing range names with any new names that match existing names. Finally, specify a range where the macro library will be inserted.

The Remove Command

Use this command to remove a macro library from memory. Remove does not erase the file from disk, and so you can load it again with Alt-*function key* **L**.

KEY SEQUENCE

Alt-<*function key*> **R** <*library*>

The Name-List Command

This command inserts into the spreadsheet a list of range names that are defined in a library. Be sure to specify a range that is empty, unless you want to overwrite data.

KEY SEQUENCE

Alt-<*function key*> **N** <*library*> <*range*>

SEE ALSO

/Add-In

The Lotus 1-2-3 Macro Command Language Keywords

This appendix contains an alphabetical listing of all the keywords in the Lotus 1-2-3 macro command language, along with the syntax of each. In the following reference entries, optional arguments are designated by enclosing them in square brackets, as in *[number]*. Required arguments appear in angle brackets. All macro keystrokes and commands must be entered as labels, which means that a macro entry must often be prefaced with an apostrophe. Braces enclose all macro keywords, and the left brace, {, is automatically interpreted as a label character; thus, macros that begin with keywords do not require the apostrophe. A macro's name is a range name consisting of a single letter from A to Z preceded by ~ (the tilde) and \ (the backslash). To execute a macro, hold down the Alt key, type the letter key by which it is named, and then release both keys. See Appendix A for information about the Macro Library Manager. For more general information on macros in Lotus 1-2-3, consult *The Complete Lotus 1-2-3 Release 2.2 Handbook* by Greg Harvey (SYBEX, 1989).

{**?**} Pauses macro execution for user input. Press Return to resume execution.

{**BEEP** *[number]*} Sounds one of the four tones used by the IBM and compatible computers, depending on the value (0–3) of its *number* argument.

{**BLANK** <*location*>} Erases the contents of a cell range.

{**BORDERSOFF**} Turns off the worksheet frame display until the macro ends or 1-2-3 reaches the next {BORDERSON} command.

{**BORDERSON**} Turns the worksheet frame display on again after it has been turned off with a {BORDERSOFF} command.

{**BRANCH** *<location>*} or **'XG**<*location*> ~ Directs execution of the macro to a new set of instructions beginning in the specified cell.

{**BREAK**} Has the same effect as pressing Ctrl-Scroll Lock.

{**BREAKOFF**} Disables the Break key (Ctrl-Scroll Lock) until the macro has completed execution or a {BREAKON} command is encountered.

{**BREAKON**} Enables the Break key (Ctrl-Scroll Lock) in a macro after it has been disabled with {BREAKOFF}.

{**CLOSE**} Closes the file previously opened with an {OPEN} statement.

{**CONTENTS** *<destination>,<source>,[width number],[format number]*} Converts a number to a label that looks like a number.

{**DEFINE** *<location1>:<type1>,<location2>:<type-2>,...*} Designates the location where each of the arguments passed to a subroutine will be stored and sets the argument type as either a value or a string.

{**DISPATCH** *<location>*} Performs indirect branching in a macro. The macro continues execution in the routine whose name appears in the specified cell.

{**FILESIZE** *<location>*} Enters the number of bytes in the currently open file into the cell address or cell range specified.

{**FOR** *<counter location>,<start number>,<stop number>,<step number>,<starting location>*} Executes a subroutine a specific number of times.

{**FORBREAK**} Immediately terminates a FOR loop, even if the stop value has not yet been reached.

{**FRAMEOFF**} Has the same effect as {BORDERSOFF}.

{**FRAMEON**} Has the same effect as {BORDERSON}.

{**GET** *<location>*} Suspends macro execution and records the first keystroke made by the user in the specified cell.

{**GETLABEL** *<prompt string>,<location>*} or **'/XL***<message>* ~ *<location>* ~ Waits for the user to enter a label (in the control panel).

{**GETNUMBER** *<prompt string>,<location>*} or **'/XN***<message>* ~ *<location>* ~ Waits for the user to enter a value (in the control panel).

{**GETPOS** *<location>*} Determines the current position of the byte pointer in the open file and returns this value in the specified cell.

{**GRAPHOFF**} Turns off graph display produced by {GRAPHON}.

{**GRAPHON** *[graph-name],[nodisplay]*} With no argument, displays current graph. The syntax {**GRAPHON** *graph-name*} displays the current graph and makes its settings the current default settings. {GRAPHON *graph-name*, **nodisplay**} makes the current graph's settings the default without displaying the graph.

{**IF** *<condition>*} or **'/XI***<condition>* ~ Evaluates the condition entered as its argument. If the condition is true, the macro continues execution in the same cell. If not, it continues execution in the cell below.

{**INDICATE** *[string]*} Places your own mode indicator in the upper-right corner of the screen, or returns to the indicator currently used by Lotus 1-2-3.

{**LET** *<location>,<number or string>*} Enters the value or label in the first cell of the range specified.

{**LOOK** *<location>*} Enters the first character currently in the typeahead buffer into the cell specified; if the buffer is empty, erases any contents of that cell.

{**MENUBRANCH** *<location>*} or **'/XM***<location>*~ Displays a custom menu in the control panel and branches to the routine chosen by the user.

{**MENUCALL** *<location>*} Displays a custom menu in the control panel and performs the subroutine call chosen by the user.

{**ONERROR** *<branch location>,[message location]*} Instructs the macro to branch to a new location and execute the instructions there when a Lotus 1-2-3 error occurs during macro execution.

{**OPEN** *<filename>*,*<access mode>*} Opens a new file for transferring data directly to or from a Lotus 1-2-3 worksheet file, depending on the *access mode* argument used.

{**PANELOFF**} Freezes the control panel in its current state during macro execution until the macro either encounters a {PANELON} statement in a subsequent command or terminates.

{**PANELON**} Reactivates the control panel after it has been frozen with a {PANELOFF} command so that it is redrawn and updated as macro execution continues.

{**PUT** *<location>*,*<col number>*,*<row number>*,*<number>*} or {**PUT** *<location>*,*<col number>*,*<row number>* ,*<string>*} Enters a number or a label at a particular location within a range.

{**QUIT**} or **'/XQ**~ Immediately terminates the execution of the macro and returns control of Lotus 1-2-3 to the user.

{**READ** *<bytecount>*,*<location>*} Transfers the number of specified bytes from the currently open ASCII file and copies them into the Lotus 1-2-3 worksheet in the cell range specified.

{**READLN** *<location>*} Transfers a single line from the currently open ASCII text file and copies it into the Lotus 1-2-3 worksheet in the cell range specified.

{**RECALC** *<location>,[condition],[iteration number]*} Recalculates all formulas in the range specified, starting with the cell in the upper left and proceeding row by row.

{**RECALCCOL** *<location>,[condition],[iteration number]*} Recalculates all the formulas in the range specified, starting with the cell in the upper left and proceeding column by column.

{**RESTART**} Clears the subroutine stack so that control is not returned to the calling routine.

{**RETURN**} or **'/XR** Immediately terminates a subroutine. The macro resumes execution with the statement just below the subroutine call statement.

{*routine name [optional argument],[optional argument],...*} or **'/XC** *location* ~ To call a subroutine in the macro, you can either enclose the name of the subroutine in curly braces, as in {*Print*} or use the '/XC command, as in *'/XCPrint&C.*

{**SETPOS** *<file position>*} Repositions the byte pointer in the currently open ASCII file.

{**SYSTEM** *command*} Pauses the macro and temporarily exits 1-2-3 to execute the specified DOS or OS/2 command. 1-2-3 and the macro resume when the operating system command is completed.

{**WAIT** *<time serial number>*} Suspends the execution of the macro until the time specified in its argument.

{**WINDOWSOFF**} Freezes the screen display until the macro encounters a {WINDOWSON} statement or terminates.

{**WINDOWSON**} Unfreezes the screen display initiated with a {WINDOWSOFF} statement, allowing the macro to redraw the screen during the rest of its execution.

{**WRITE** <*string*>} Directly transfers a string of characters from the Lotus 1-2-3 worksheet to an open ASCII file at the current position in that file.

{**WRITELN** <*string*>} Transfers a string of characters from the Lotus 1-2-3 worksheet to an open ASCII file at the current position in that file; also adds carriage-return and line-feed characters to the end of the string to mark the end of the line.

Index

Command Index

Function Index

Subject Index